Lifting the Cup

Lifting the Cup

The Story of Battling Barnsley
1910–12

Mark Metcalf and David Wood

First published in Great Britain in 2010 by
Wharncliffe Books
an imprint of
Pen and Sword Books Limited,
47 Church Street, Barnsley,
South Yorkshire S70 2AS

Copyright © Mark Metcalf and David Wood, 2010

ISBN: 978 1 84563 1 369

The right of Mark Metcalf and David Wood to be identified
as authors of this work has been asserted by them in accordance
with the Copyright, Designs and Patents Act, 1988.

A CIP catalogue record of this book is available
from the British Library.

Printed and bound in Great Britain by CPI UK

Pen & Sword Books Ltd incorporates the imprints of
Pen & Sword Aviation, Pen & Sword Maritime,
Pen & Sword Military, Wharncliffe Local History, Pen & Sword Select,
Pen & Sword Military Classics, Leo Cooper, Remember When,
Seaforth Publishing and Frontline Publishing

For a complete list of Pen & Sword titles please contact:
PEN & SWORD BOOKS LIMITED
47 Church Street, Barnsley, South Yorkshire, S70 2AS, England.
E-mail: enquiries@pen-and-sword.co.uk
Website: www.pen-and-sword.co.uk

Contents

DEDICATION

This book is dedicated to Wilfred Bartrop, who was tragically killed in action on 7 November 1918, just four days before the end of World War One.

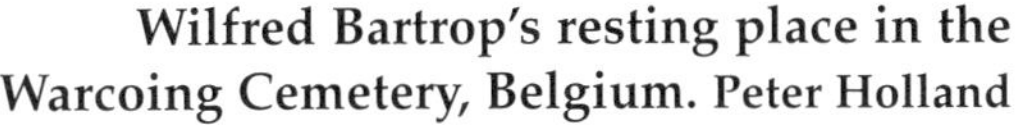

Wilfred Bartrop's resting place in the Warcoing Cemetery, Belgium. Peter Holland

Editor's Introduction

This is the second book that I have commissioned and edited relating to Barnsley Football Club (the other being *Barnsley's Greatest Games* by Grenville Firth, Wharncliffe Books, 2009). This publication is a very appropriate one since it is 'made in Barnsley' and appears a century after the start of the 1910 FA Cup campaign in which Battling Barnsley reached the Final. It concludes with the magnificent cup win of 1912 and a 'Champions of the World' title.

We are also indebted to the authors for providing us with a considerable amount of background information concerning the early years of the Club and its remarkable European Tour of 1910.

The detailed pen-portraits of Barnsley FC's 'Cup Heroes' also provide us with a fascinating insight into the lives of the manager, trainer and players, an invaluable source of reference for many years to come.

Mark Metcalf and David Wood have done an excellent job in their research and writing; and the assembling of so many supporting images, many of them rare and unpublished, is a tremendous achievement. Wherever possible the authors have given credit to copyright and picture collection holders, their contributions much appreciated. In order to compare past and present monetary values I am very grateful for the use of the currency conversion facility from The National Archives.

Brian Elliott

Acknowledgements

The authors would like to acknowledge the following people who have contributed in some part to the finished article that is this book.

Firstly we would like to extend our gratitude to the Barnsley FC owner Patrick Cryne for the support he has given us during the compilation of this book and to Barry Taylor for kindly agreeing to provide the Foreword.

Our thanks go to Arthur Bower who was until February 2009 the Official Historian to Barnsley Football Club. He is a living connection to the winning of the Cup as both his father and grandfather were at Bramall Lane to see Barnsley's triumph, and throughout the time of this project he has made his collection of postcards and photographs available. This has enabled us to produce the most comprehensive display of Barnsley related images from the era ever assembled. Also we are indebted to local sporting author and Barnsley fan Grenville Firth for providing an array of team groups and postcards and for the loan of a file of match reports which saved us untold months of searching in the library. We were very fortunate to have the official historians of both Newcastle United and West Bromwich Albion available to contribute the pen portraits of Barnsley's Cup Final opponents. For this we thank Paul Joannou and Tony Matthews respectively.

Furthermore we would like to mention the reporters of yesteryear for their words and enthusiasm. The contributors of many match reports are lost in the annals of time but the work of 'Argus' and 'Centre Forward' from the *Barnsley Independent* is prevalent throughout this book. Also, without the extensive letters sent home from Peter Waite, a Barnsley director and the landlord of the Clarence Hotel, the European Tour section just could not have been written.

Finally we would like to heartily thank the following who have played a part in this publication: commissioning and series editor Brian Elliott and the staff of Pen and Sword Books; the staff of Barnsley Library and Archives; the staff of Manchester Central Library; Paul Days; Bryn Owen; Linzi Henry; Peter Holland; Peter Holme; Derek Hyde and Don Wearmouth.

Foreword

It gives me great pleasure to write the Foreword to this book about our club's glorious past. I was born at the top of Dodworth Bottom and like numerous others down the years, Barnsley is my team and football is my game. I don't think I ever had much choice in either matter nor did I want one. My town, my team, my blood. Now where have I read that before?

The game of football has been very good to me. It has allowed me to captain my town in front of 20,000 at Oakwell in the English Schools final of 1957, to sign amateur forms at the club I love a year later, to become a director of the same club in 1986 and finally, as chairman of the FA Cup Committee, to see my team come within ninety minutes of a third FA Cup Final. All these moments have filled me with immense pride as, through the medium of football, I have represented my town on a national stage. In later years, I have become a member of the International Committee and a UEFA delegate and no matter where I travel on duty with my country, it fills me with an equal amount of pride to find out they all know about Barnsley FC.

As a football fan (and I've been watching Barnsley for over sixty years) you are always waiting in anticipation for the next game. If we've won the previous week, can the run continue? If we've lost, can we get back to winning ways? Sometimes we can get wrapped up in the 'now' and forget to take stock of our previous successes. The feeling we had when we won promotion to the Premier League in 1997 or after the Play-off Final in Cardiff is still there somewhere inside us all and we must never forget our history, as it has made the club and the people we are.

With this in mind I must pass on my congratulations to Mark Metcalf and David Wood for bringing the story of our greatest triumph alive. As every Barnsley supporter will know, we won the FA Cup in 1912 and the scorer of the winning goal was Harry Tufnell. Now, for the first time in one book, we can follow the team's progress from disappointment to success against the news stories of the day.

Barry Taylor
Director
Barnsley Football Club

Introduction

Barnsley Football Club were formed in 1887, entered the Football League in 1898, and at the start of the 1909-10 season were facing their twelfth season in Division 2 under the direction of Manager/Secretary Arthur Fairclough.

Having finished in seventeenth place the previous season, and with little in the way of finances to spend on new players, there was little to suggest that the club's most illustrious and successful period was just around the corner. Yet over the next three seasons a magnificent Barnsley side thrilled their supporters by winning their way through to the FA Cup Final, then the most prestigious cup tournament in the World, on not one but two occasions and capped things off by beating West Bromwich Albion in the 1912 Final to capture the FA Cup for the only time, so far, in the club's history. We should also not forget they became the first English side to avoid defeat in the 'Championship of the World' by drawing at the home of Celtic, the winners of the Scottish Cup, at the commencement of the 1912-13 season.

One hundred years on, this book brings to life through match reports, photographs (some never previously seen before) and memorabilia the matches and excitement of these momentous times that included the extraordinary commitment shown by some Barnsley fans to see their side in the FA Cup. Against a background of major social and political change, this book also examines the players who made history and became legends in their own right.

PART ONE

FOOTBALL IN 1910

Whilst a form of football has probably existed for as long as men have had feet with which to kick things, the game as we know it today was under a hundred years old in 1910.

Various forms of football had come into being in the major public schools during the second or third decade of the nineteenth century. However, the first attempts to unify the different strands and establish a unified system of rules failed in 1848.

There was more success in 1862 and in November that year a match at Cambridge took place between Cambridge Old Etonians and Cambridge Old Harrovians on a level playing field under a set of rules that almost 150 years later most football fans could recognise. Happily, the rules, which included eleven players on each side, worked and the revised Cambridge rules of 1863 became the basis for the first laws of the Football Association (FA) that was formed on 26 October 1863.

Within eight years, on 11 November 1871, the first ever matches in the longest running competitive football competition in the world took place when eight sides lined up in the FA Cup. Its success and that of the first international matches that followed soon led to the establishment of a Football League (later First Division or Division 1) in 1888 with twelve clubs.

With more and more clubs seeking entry, a second league was formed in season 1892-93, as football's popularity as a spectator sport increased across the country, leading to an increasingly professional sport.

Although Scottish side Queens Park are believed to have been the first side to have recognised the value of 'letting the ball do the work', it is Preston North End, as winners of the first two championships, who are credited with inventing the passing game. This brought with it the need to adopt team formations for both attack and defence leading to the 2-3-5 set up of two full backs, three half backs and five forwards.

The key player in this was the centre-half who would be expected to surge forward in support of his forwards and it was usual for most sides to play their most creative player in this key position. It was to be 1925 before the role of the centre-half changed when the offside law was altered after concerns about how few goals were being scored. It meant that players could now be onside if there were only two players between themselves and their opponents' goal rather than three.

There were no such things as substitutes in 1910, so if a player got injured he was usually required to limp out the match on the (left) wing. There was no such thing as advertising on strips, and numbering on the shirts was a good thirty years away. The ball used was rock hard and when it got wet it could become a very heavy object that also went out of shape. Player's boots had studs hammered into the soles.

Without adequate drainage systems pitches bore no similarity to the fabulous billiard table-like surfaces of the Premier League today and had little grass on them, especially in the winter. Heavy rain brought puddles for the players to overcome, and on particularly rainy days the middle of the pitch would soon resemble a mud bath. This made it essential for teams to get the ball out to their wingers to attack the full-backs.

One other significant difference compared with today is also that in 1910 goalkeepers were allowed to handle the ball anywhere in their own half. If that might have made it easier for the men between the sticks what didn't was the rule that allowed them to be shoulder charged, just like any other player, with or without the ball.

A HISTORY OF BARNSLEY FOOTBALL CLUB TO 1910

1 Early Days

The successes that Barnsley Football Club was to enjoy in 1910 and 1912 were only made possible by the dedication of the club officials, players and staff that went before them. Together, in less than quarter of a century, they established a club in a rugby stronghold, developed a ground to accommodate an increasing number of spectators, successfully applied to join the Football League and put the club in a position to challenge for honours, of which none was greater than the FA Cup.

The earliest record of football being played in Barnsley was of 'A Great Football Match' on Market Hill in August 1790. It caused the closure of the local tradesmen's shops and was most probably similar in style and confusion to the massed scrum games that have survived to this day in Ashbourne, Workington and Kirkwall. It also appears to have been a one-off with no details of a rematch being recorded by the local press.

As such it was Rugby which became the most popular sporting code in the town, and although Barnsley were by the far the strongest of the local rugby clubs, Barnsley Parish and Barnsley Cons also received more than a liberal patronage from the local sporting public. All of this was to the detriment of the strongest of the local Association Clubs of which Barnsley Wanderers were probably the most successful.

Wanderers in fact were to provide the first Barnsley man to be recognised for representative honours. This came when goalkeeper Arthur Mallinson was selected for the annual Sheffield v Glasgow fixture in 1882. Such was his performance between the sticks in the victory at Bramall Lane that the on-rushing spectators chaired him from the field to the dressing rooms. Nevertheless, like several other Association clubs that also came into existence in the town, namely Casuals, Victoria, White Lilly and Farriers, Mallinson's club failed to capture the imagination of the Barnsley public and received meagre support.

Club founder, Reverend Tiverton Preedy.
Wood Collection

So it was against this trend and the thoughts of the locals that a 'Football' team would never thrive in Barnsley, that the curate to St Peter's Church, Mr Tiverton Preedy (he abhorred his religious title of 'Reverend') decided to try to buck the trend. He had arrived in Barnsley as a wholehearted Rugby enthusiast and player, but a disagreement with the Barnsley Club over the arrangement of a fixture on Good Friday saw him resign his position and look to form his own team around his church. 'We will start an association club such as the Rugbyites will not crush' are his words spoken to friends prior to the formation of the club but when it got around the town about his intentions, he met with more ridicule than support for identifying himself with such a task.

Yet Tiverton Preedy was no fool, football was on the rise in every part of the country and the Football League was only a year in the making. The FA Cup was already into its second decade and professionalism was on the march.

As such, the success of the inaugural meeting of the Barnsley St Peter's club on 8 September 1887 meant that just some eleven days later the club played their first fixture at Ward Green against Manor House. The eleven players to represent the Saints were: goal, J.Mason; backs, G Walker and R Chappell; half-backs, K Armitage, J Beckett and S Harrison; forwards, Rev T Preedy, A Thompson, S Denton, S Thompson and A Harrison. The club won handsomely 4-1 with Steven Denton (2), R Chappell and A Thompson the club's first goal scorers. All, of course, are long gone but without them one of the best known football clubs in England would not be looking forward to celebrating its 125th anniversary in 2012. And it was these men, who speaking in 1910 prior to the FA Cup final, Mr Preedy recalled:

The pioneers of soccer at St Peter's were a band of young men. They didn't trouble about 'gates', what they wanted were goals. Spectators

Believed to be the earliest (c.1887) image of the Barnsley St Peter's team. An interesting feature of the of the maroon and navy shirts is that they carry numbers on their fronts, possibly the first known example in the world. **Bower Collection**

could come and were welcome. The lads were pleased to see them. But hey did not In anyway depend on them. Our success was by no means stantaneous. Rugger was the game up to then and the new style met ith in strenuous opposition. The Press, the people, everyone seemed to be against us, but we fought on. I might add that the first time we made a collection we got 2s 6^1/2d [12.5p]. Before I left for London the club was firmly on its feet, nor does it seem to have come to any harm through losing me!

In 1887, St Peter's moved quickly to secure a playing enclosure and was lucky to find an ally in Mr Guy Senior a local landowner. After several refusals, he finally bowed to the Reverend's pressure and agreed to rent the field adjoining the current pitch at Oakwell to the club. He must have had slight reservations about 'Preedy's Boys', as the transaction came with a humorous stipulation to save Mr Senior from any association with wrong doing, stating, 'You can have the field so long as you behave yourselves.'

The first season consisted only of friendlies and the make-up of the team slowly changed as better players came along. By the halfway stage of the campaign five players had joined who would go on to give stalwart service in later seasons. Tom Hirst, 'Con' Needham, 'Flick' Beevors and Billy Berry all left local opposition to throw in their lot with the Saints while Tom Nixon would make it all the way to play in the Football League for Barnsley in 1898.

The programme for the second season was more ambitious than the first and although still confined to friendly matches, the club entered the Sheffield Challenge Cup for the first time. Hopes of initial cup-tie glory though were rudely cut short by Staveley Town who hammered the Saints 12-0, to inflict what still remains the club's record defeat.

It was during this season that Joseph Raley, an old Wanderers player and later to become the town's Mayor, joined as a player and enthusiastic supporter of the club. He was quickly appointed captain on the field and gave many sterling performances but it was his actions off the field that were more telling. An astute orator and organiser, the rapid progress made by the club in later seasons can be attributed largely to his efforts as secretary and chairman.

In the third and final season of friendly fixtures the club had a fine record winning twenty-two out of thirty-two games. This success, including a 13-0 home victory over Leeds Steelworks, encouraged the Saints to join the likes of Kilnhurst, Ecclesfield and Mexborough in the Sheffield & District League.

After finishing in a respectable sixth position in their first season, a third place finish in the second was compounded by reaching the semi-finals of the Sheffield Cup and the final of the newly offered Barnsley Charity Cup. The latter game was played at the Shaw Lane Cricket ground and in front of the largest crowd ever to see a football match in Barnsley, raised receipts of £76. The Saints were supremely confident of carrying off the prize and booked a band to accompany the victorious team from the ground to the reception at the King's

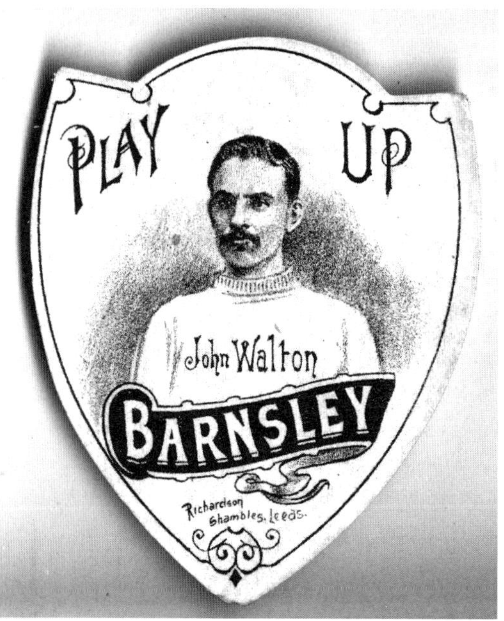

This is the earliest representation of a Barnsley player on a commercial trade card. John Walton was the St Peter's goalkeeper in season 1991-2. Wood Collection

Head Hotel but their opponents Ecclesfield proved too clever and ran out 3-1 winners. The unexpected result was to have deep repercussions on the club and its history and many hard things were said at its conclusion, including an unfounded allegation that the goalkeeper had thrown the game. Indeed the sight of the procession marching through the town to the strains of *See the conquering heroes come*, with Ecclesfield at its head, did little to console the Saints' officials who'd had their team in special training for a whole week.

The following season, 1892-3, was far from successful but was noted for the club's efforts to bring in fresh talent from further afield. Through the alertness of Reverend Preedy no fewer than six players of the victorious Ecclesfield side were engaged, along with Alec Black who joined the club after coming to the town as a schoolteacher.

Once again the final of the Barnsley Cup was reached where it took two games to resolve the tie with rivals Mexborough. The games were played at the Queens Ground and the great local excitement created showed how quickly the popularity of the game was growing. Mr JC Clegg, the chairman of the FA, acted as referee and a special stand was erected on the low side of the upper part of the ground. The first encounter was a 1-1 draw with fully 6,000 spectators present and the replay on the following Thursday saw the Saints triumph 4-1 in front of a crowd of 7,000-8,000.

Before the season closed, Reverend Preedy severed his connection with the club to take up clerical duties in London. The players presented him with a walking stick, pipe and pouch while the Barnsley Football Union gave a purse of £60. He always maintained a keen interest in the club and prior to every FA Cup game until his death in 1928 he would send a telegram of encouragement.

In 1893-4 the club appeared in the FA Cup for the first time, losing 5-4 at home to Gainsborough Trinity in controversial circumstances. Barnsley officials claimed one of the visitor's scores was punched into the net and an injury time equaliser was denied after the referee failed to spot the ball crossing the line. They had a tolerable season in the Sheffield League gaining fourth position and retained the Barnsley Cup by beating Wombwell Town. Such was the progressive spirit in the club that it was suggested that the club apply to join the Midland League but it was felt that the team had hardly attained the proper status to justify any application.

Season 1894-5 saw many changes in the team line-up, including the arrival of Spurley Hey from Stocksbridge, Vost from West Manchester and Partridge from Birdwell. The highlight of the season was the progress made in the FA Cup with the first round proper being reached for the first time in the club's history. Liverpool were drawn at Oakwell but quickly laid an objection to the ground, owing to its alleged unsuitability. Certainly the conditions left much

Joseph Greaves,
Barnsley.

Ogden's Cigarettes.

Joseph Greaves joined the club prior to the 1893-4 season and went on to be the regular choice between the sticks for the next ten years. He figured throughout the club's Sheffield and Midland League days and became the first Barnsley footballer to appear in 100 Football League games. Wood Collection

to be desired, for the playing pitch was not fully enclosed. However, the objection failed on technical grounds having been presented too late to the FA. The attitude of the Liverpool officials engendered the game with much keenness, and although the ground was covered with a considerable depth of snow, the attendance numbered some 5,000.

Barnsley undoubtedly deserved to win, but at the end of 90 minutes the teams were locked at one goal each. The referee persisted in ordering extra time to be played, though Barnsley protested this to be illegal, as the rule at the time specified this could only be done with the consent of both teams. Liverpool scored the 'winning' goal during the closing stages of the last period but at the end of the game the referee admitted his misinterpretation of the rule and the authorities ordered a replay at Liverpool which the home side won comfortably 4-0.

Despite the setback, the receipts from the cup run allowed the club to make a small surplus on the season even when allowing for the construction of a small covered stand on the topside of the ground. This construction had created much interest and consisted of a three-terraced erection with a corrugated iron back and roof, but it had not been up long when one night during a violent gale, it was blown over bodily into the field of play.

In the summer of 1895 the club successful applied to the Midland League and an arrangement was made for the reserves to play in the Barnsley Football Union. To meet these challenges, the club raised admission prices from 3d to 4d (1-2p) and set about recruiting several new players for the campaign including the stalwart Donald Lees from Lincoln City.

An early exit from the FA Cup reduced the interest around the town and with league match gate receipts averaging only £10, the financial position was one of anxiety for the committee. Notices were served to the players (including Lees who had shown undoubted ability) with a view to reducing expenditure and members of the finance committee were suspended until the season's end for alleged illegal payments to players. On the field, the winning of the Wharncliffe Cup was the lone success in an uneventful season.

Several notable players took their departure during the following season including Nixon, Tyas, Rogers, Lees and Fred Woolhouse but favourable success in the Cup enabled the club to retrieve their precarious financial position. In an earlier round the Saints beat Football League opposition for the only time in their non-league days with a 2-1 victory at Lincoln City and had the reward of a home tie against First Division Derby County to consider.

No sooner did Derby know their fate that they made overtures to switch the game to the Baseball Ground and, partly owing to the state of the Oakwell pitch, the committee accepted the proposal. The deal was £100, half the gate receipts and a friendly at a later date. Barnsley came away from the cup-tie with a cheque for £181 (worth £10,840 today) and an 8-1 thumping for their troubles.

When the annual meeting came around, and with the knowledge that Barnsley Rugby Club had collapsed there was a renewed attempt to alter the name of the club to Barnsley Association Football Club. Those behind the move felt that it would show that this was now 'the town's club' and those present agreed. It was also a fact that with the exception of the club's president Mr Preedy there was no longer any association with St Peter's Church and severance from the name lifted the ban on games being played on Good Friday, the very act that ten years previously had led to the formation of the club.

2 Joining the Football League

No sooner had the 1896-7 season finished than information began to circulate regarding the team-building for the forthcoming campaign. The most important and appreciative statement concerned the return to Oakwell of Tom Nixon and Don Lees from Darwin. Dave Porteous, a back from Rotherham, was secured along with the left wing partnership of McCullough and Jones from Liverpool White Star; and later in the season Harry Davis joined the Oakwell throng for a £5 fee from Ardsley.

Although Barnsley met with an early departure in the FA Cup at old rivals Mexborough, the team put up a strong fight for the championship of the Midland League with the crucial game at the home of their Dearne Valley neighbours. Backed by some 2,000 followers, the men from Oakwell were unable to avoid defeat and this, coupled with a final day defeat at Rushden, handed the title to Mexborough.

The effort shown to attain the Midland League flag nevertheless encouraged those club members who favoured seeking admission to the Football League to press their point. Many considered the application to be premature but the committee recommended it to their members and a majority of one saw the motion passed. On reflection, the committee decided that this was too important a decision to be swayed by a single vote and called a special meeting that saw the proposal unanimously carried and a guaranteed fund of £200 (c. £11,978 today) was raised from the room. Initially Barnsley found they were competing for three available places and did not receiving a single nomination vote as Lincoln City, Loughborough and Burslem Port Vale were duly elected.

But sometime after the meeting, the League decided to increase its divisions to eighteen clubs each and would be requiring an extra four clubs. Darwen were assured of their place without the need of a ballot and a close contest saw Barnsley elected in third place behind New Brighton Tower and Glossop North End. However, there were certain conditions attached to the elevation namely the provision of dressing rooms so that players and officials would be able to leave the field of play without interference. These alterations were largely carried out by voluntary labour at a cost of about £170 and also involved moving some 3,000 cubic feet of soil from one corner of the ground to the other in an attempt to level the pitch, the covering of the existing stand and the erection of an uncovered stand on the bottom side of the ground.

3 Division Two Football

A number of players were signed prior to the club's first season in the Football League, the most prominent being the experienced John McCartney who was made club captain. For the first game, a 1-0 defeat at Lincoln City, the club were represented by the following team: Fawcett; Nixon, McCartney; Burleigh, King, Porteous; Davis, Lees, Murray, McCullough and McGee. McCartney scored the club's first goal with a penalty in a 2-1 win over Luton Town some days later and although the club were to beat Small Heath 7-2 and see a 9-0 record victory over Loughborough in the season, a finishing position of 11th was considered disappointing. Incidentally, the 9-0 success saw Barnsley wear red shirts for the first time. They changed from their blue and white stripes to avoid clashing with their visitors and the success on the field saw the new shirts adopted as the home strip. Off the field the financial position was also far from satisfactory with a season's end deficit of £450 being reached.

The following season saw the club experiment with entering the first team in the Midland League as well as the Second Division, but after a record of just thirteen victories from the 54 fixtures it could hardly be called a success. A bad start to the League campaign was never fully recovered and a bottom three finish meant the club had to apply for re-election with the known fact that if the pitch was not improved its brief league career was over. So amid a worsening financial situation, the unanimous returning vote carried with it a millstone of improvements valued at around £400. The overdraft at the bank stood at £578 (c. £34,616 today), despite the £175 transfer of Harry Davis to Sheffield Wednesday. To reduce the liabilities on the club's officials important changes had to be made.

It was decided to form the club into a limited company with capital of £1,000 in 10s shares and local businesses and the public were invited to contribute but the response was very poor. Directors even resorted to going door to door to sell the shares and despite their enthusiasm only £500 were purchased with the remainder being covered by the chairman Mr Fred Senior. Commenting in 1910, those who had worked to keep the club alive at this time 'could never forget how tradesmen were so blind to their own interests in their stolid indifference as to whether the club continued or not'.

A card from 1907, issued by Scissors cigarettes in India, showing Barnsley's colours at the time. Wood Collection

It was within the first month of the 1900-01 season that an injury befell John McCartney which caused his retirement from the game and in other respects the season proved disappointing. The support of the public was very moderate, with a continued run of defeats, and the position had become such that some players returned the whole or part of their week's wages to assist the club. The club also came close to a successive re-election application that may have not been seen so favourably as the previous years vote. In the final match of the season they pulled a point clear of the zone which left an anxious wait of a few days for Walsall to complete their fixtures. The resulting draw by the 'Saddlers' meant the club survived by the margin of goal average the possibility of leaving the League.

The later success of the Reds in this decade has its foundations firmly placed in the summer of 1901 when Arthur Fairclough resigned as secretary of the club and John McCartney was appointed secretary-manager. This was the first time that one man would have control over player and team selection but the directors knew of their popular captain and felt this was the right man in the right role.

His first task was the signing of players who could perform in the club's fourth season of League football and for this purpose he set out for Scotland in search of 'new blood'. A few weeks later he returned with the news that over ten new players had been secured at an outlay of less than £10 (worth c. £570 today). The much changed team took quite some time to settle down and the dread of re-election was again more than a possibility. Entering February, the club were in the bottom three but a run of just three defeats in the next thirteen games saw a respectable 11th place achieved and only four clubs scored more

First row :—T. Pleasant (Director), W. Wood (Director), W. Cutts (Trainer), H. E. Bennett (right half), West (full back), William McCartney (centre half)
J. Greaves (goal), A. Oxspring (right half), C. Welsh (full back) J. McCartney (Secretary and Manager), F. B. Bedford (Director), T. H. Fisher.
Second row :— J. Lang (outside right), F. Cornan (inside right), A. Hellewell (centre), A. Underwood (inside left), R. Bourne (outside left).
BARNSLEY.
Photographed by F. B. Bedford, Barnsley.

The Barnsley team in 1902-03. Wood Collection

goals throughout the campaign.

During the close season 'Mac' was enthusiastic, along with a willing band of workers, in erecting useful shelters on the popular side of the ground in the hope that larger attendances could be secured on wet days and lots of other work was undertaken to generally improve the enclosure. On the field, the season proved to be the most successful to date with a final league position of eighth and Aston Villa being drawn at Oakwell for a second round FA Cup clash. The still precarious financial position saw the game switched to Villa Park for £250 and half of any gate receipts and four trains full of Barnsley fans took advantage of subsidised travel to attend the game. The club pocketed around £650 (c.£37,000 today) from the fixture, which nearly equated to the profit on the season and saw the overdraft cleared at the bank for the first time in many a year.

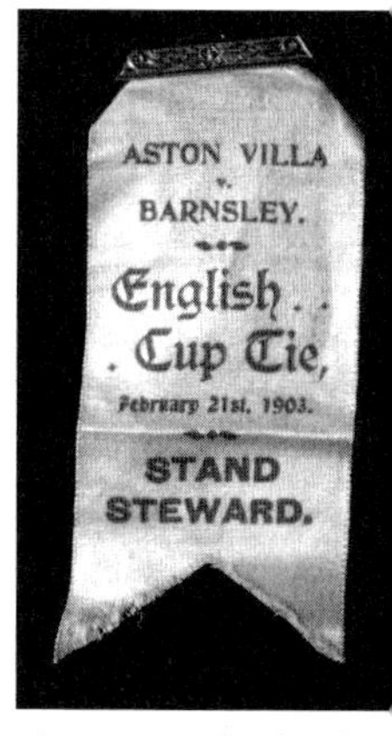

A steward's badge
Wood Collection

A big effort to improve the drainage of Oakwell took place prior to the 1903-04 season with large quantities of rock and clay being removed from the topside of the ground and over 1,600 yards of new turf being laid. New dressing rooms were built this time equipped with baths and other facilities, and quite a number of useful players were added to the squad. In October, it was felt that the club were so strong in reserve talent that they would listen to offers for its better players. Benny Green was a natural goal scorer and a rare talent, but he had failed to find the net in any of that season's games so the club felt the sum of £500 was fair recompense for his services. The acceptance of £500 from Liverpool for Alf West a fortnight later set the club on a sound financial footing and despite these departures the club finished again in a credible eighth position.

The following season began with the resignation of John McCartney who had accepted the position of secretary-manager at St Mirren football club. It had not been plain sailing for Mac for some time but he had the satisfaction of leaving the club both on and off the field in probably their best ever position.

4 Arthur Fairclough

Arthur Fairclough was induced to fill the position and promptly signed a selection of new players for the club. The financial position had allowed the club to build a new covered stand (still present today) on the top side of the ground. The structure cost £600 (c.£34,400 today), could accommodate 1,200 spectators and was formally opened by the Mayor prior to the first home game of the campaign. Also October saw the erection at the ground of the largest half-time scoreboard in England. Built in conjunction with the agency that supplied the results, the structure was the only one big enough to display the scores from both divisions continuously. On the field the season proved to be a fairly successful one with an all-time high of seventh position being attained and an increase in gate receipts on the previous year.

1905-6 was to prove another financially successful season, but the following campaign proved to be one of the most remarkable in the club's short history. Two of the greatest goal-scorers ever to play for Barnsley, Jackie Mordue and George Reeves, were brought together halfway through the season to transform the fortunes of the club. At the beginning of December the club were placed just one point from the bottom of the table but a run of five defeats in the remaining twenty-three games saw an eighth place finish with a record number of goals scored. In the FA Cup even greater success was obtained, despite the absence of Mordue and Reeves who were both cup-tied. After a draw and subsequent victory over Nottingham Forest, Portsmouth, who were drawn next at Oakwell, tried to transfer the game to the south coast. The directors declined the offer and promptly doubled admission prices with little opposition from the public. Bury were then despatched in the third round

The 1907 'English Cup Team', a montage for a postcard produced by local photographer George Washington Irving. Wood Collection

leaving First Division Woolwich Arsenal between Barnsley and a place in the semi-finals. All four home games of the cup run had delivered record crowds and record receipts but a surprise victory for the Londoners put paid to any dreams of glory. At the season's end, with finances healthy, a number of players were transferred from the club, including Mordue, who joined Arsenal for the maximum figure allowed of £450. As in previous years, any surplus on the season had been used towards ground improvements and this season's excess of £1,500 (c. £86,000 today) was put towards a ground fund but the supporters were dismayed at the sale of their stars without due cause.

The succeeding season of 1907-8 was in direct contrast to the previous campaign. Yet in spite of the loss of Mordue, Stacey and Brookes, the club made a satisfactory start. Then came the bombshell that having scored fourteen goals in twelve games Reeves was to be sold to Aston Villa for a record fee and all hope for the season was broken. The subsequent games yielded poor returns and only a very hard struggle prevented the club slipping into the bottom three and having to apply for re-election. Even the news that the club had secured their long-term target of the freehold of Oakwell and its surrounds did little to cheer the crowds. They knew a successful team had been asset stripped and for the first time in many years it looked as if the club were going backwards.

The directors knew they were up against it with the Barnsley public and had to do something to gain their patronage. Prior to the start of the 1908-9 season they announced the club had 'engaged the most likely set of men who have ever worn the Oakwell colours' and indeed they brought in the likes of Jackie Cooper, Dickie Downs and Harry Ness to complement the team.

Prior to this season, only Tommy Boyle, Tom Forman and George Lillycrop had secured regular games but within the squad George Utley and Bob Glendenning were developing as players and had already tasted League Football. Several of these men were to show such excellent form later but the opening of the season was far from promising with only eight points being gained from a possible thirty-two. Boyle and Glendenning were moved into the half-back line and an all round pull together from December onwards, entirely based on home form, saw the club only just escape re-election. The away form remained woeful with only seven points and no victories recorded for the season but George Lillycrop proved one of the few successes by scoring a record equalling nineteen goals from centre forward.

THE 1909-10 SEASON

1 The campaign up to the start of the cup-run

Tommy Thorpe was the only major departure when, prior to the start of 1909-10 season, officials failed to come to terms with the popular keeper. Mearns was signed as goalkeeping back-up to Cooper along with young forward Gadsby, speedy winger Bartrop and the man later go on to win the cup for Barnsley, Harry Tufnell. From the second game of the season when Bartrop was selected, Barnsley had a settled outfield side that would see them throughout the season and to the Cup Final. Once again the home form was awesome with the twelve games prior to the cup run yielding ten wins and one draw with just the opening day defeat with Hull City to spoil the record. In October, the club recorded back-to-back seven-goal hauls with the 7-0 victory

Barnsley FC's 'Playing Staff' in 1909-10. Bower Collection

at Leeds proving to be Barnsley's solitary success on their travels. In December an injury to Jackie Cooper allowed Mearns to take his chance between the sticks and, as the campaign developed, the injured keeper made several attempted comebacks. This even included the playing of two cup-ties but he could not dislodge his understudy. Mearns had to be satisfied with playing the many midweek games which came around due to the cup success.

2 The FA Cup before 1910

The old FA Cup trophy.
Wood Collection

The FA Cup is the longest running football tournament in the World. It kicked off on 11 November 1871 when eight teams took part in the first truly competitive football matches as a prize awaited the competition winners. The organisation behind it were the Football Association, hence the FA Cup. They had been formed in 1863 'with the object of establishing a definite code of rules for the regulation of the game'.

On the evening of 20 July 20 1871, their secretary, Charles William Alcock, proposed 'that a Challenge Cup should be established" was accepted and the FA Cup was thus born. Alcock was to live to see the first Wembley final in 1923, dying aged ninety-three the following year.

The first final, at Kennington Oval, was contested between the Wanderers and Royal Engineers on 16 March 1872. Wanderers' success, the first of five, came from a single goal scored by Morton Peto Betts. Around 2,000 people paid one shilling (5p, about £2.30 today) to watch the match.

In 1889, following the launch of the Football League the previous season, Preston North End became the first side to do 'the double', capturing the Division 1 title and the FA Cup. Aston Villa joined them in the record books in 1897.

In 1901, Tottenham became the first, and only, non-League side to win the FA Cup, beating the favourites Sheffield United in a replay 3-1, with the first match having attracted more than 110,000 people.

Cup kings in 1910 were undoubtedly Blackburn Rovers who had captured the trophy on five occasions with wins in 1884, 1885, 1886, 1890 and 1891. Rovers' three wins in a row equalled that of The Wanderers between 1876 and 1878.

In comparison, Barnsley had a chequered cup history, their sixteen previous attempts on the trophy yielding just one quarter-final place, a 2-1 home defeat to Woolwich Arsenal in 1907.

Cup holders were Manchester United, victors for the first time courtesy of a Sandy Turnbull effort after 22 minutes against Bristol City in a match played at the Crystal Palace. Wembley, of course, was not to open until 1923. Having won the First Division title in three of the last six seasons, Newcastle United were one of the favourites to win the FA Cup and were determined to make up for cup final defeats in 1905, 1906 and 1908.

The FA Cup proper in 1909-10 consisted of four rounds, the semi-finals, and the final. However, even before the first round there were two preliminary rounds. The first featured forty teams with the twenty winners lining up with a further 244 teams for the right to qualify for the first of five qualifying rounds, at the end of which the twelve non-League Clubs still standing were joined by teams from the first and second divisions of which Barnsley were one. The FA Cup proper kicked off on 15 January 1910.

3 FA Cup First Round v Blackpool

Saturday 15 January 1910: Bloomfield Road, Blackpool

Blackpool   1 (Wolstenholme)
Barnsley   1 (Tufnell)
Attendance: 8,000

Barnsley were lying in eighth place in Division II when they kicked off their 1910 campaign at Blackpool, sitting just one place below in the league. The Tykes were buoyed by an impressive performance at home the previous weekend when promotion-chasing Glossop North End were beaten 3-0 with two goals from Lillycrop, bringing his season's total to eighteen so far, and one from Boyle. However, with only one victory from nine away league games, a 7-0 win at Leeds City in October, they were bound to face a stern examination if they were to progress.

Although it was pouring with rain, it failed to dampen the enthusiasm of thousands of the club's supporters, who had traveled by special trains, when the teams ran out on a mud-soaked Bloomfield Road pitch on 15 January 1910. At stake was a place in the FA Cup second round.

Considering the conditions, the match proved to be a fine affair, with both sides straining every muscle in a hard fought no holds barred contest that was never allowed to get out control thanks to some excellent refereeing by Mr I Baker of Nantwich. At the end, although Barnsley had probably been the better side, few of those present could quibble with the result especially as 'the Seasiders' had played part of the 90 minutes with only ten men.

The players at Lytham St Annes prior to the 1st round cup tie against Blackpool, January 1910. Back row: Downs, Mearns, Ness; Middle row: Glendenning, Boyle, Utley; front-row: Bartrop, Gadsby, Lillycrop, Tufnell, Forman; extreme left: Norman (trainer).
Bower Collection

There were already puddles of water on the pitch when the referee's whistle got the game under way. Blackpool were without their skipper Jack Cox from the earlier league game with Barnsley that had finished 1-1. From the start the away side pressed but found the Blackpool keeper Bill Fiske in fine form, sliding out on more than one occasion to grab the ball as the Barnsley forwards searched for the opening goal.

This eventually came when Lillycrop showed great unselfishness by ignoring a shooting chance to push the ball out to Tufnell standing just inside the penalty area on the left. In a flash the Barnsley inside-left had weighed up his options and blasted the ball past Fiske to make it Blackpool 0 Barnsley 1.

Things looked even rosier for the away team when PA Goulding was carried off the field with concussion following a clash thus reducing Blackpool to ten men in an era when substitutes were never even considered. Yet despite enjoying almost unlimited possession for the rest of the first 45 minutes Barnsley never really looked like adding to their total.

Blackpool were no doubt heartened by the reappearance of Goulding after half-time and searched frantically for an equaliser. According to the Independent's reporter at the match Utley and Ness were guilty in the second period of allowing Blackpool's right winger identified in the match report as 'the amateur BJ [Sid] Hoade' too much room thus allowing him 'openings for some good and dangerous centres'.

The equaliser from Arthur Wolstenholme was unstoppable, striking the angle of the bar and flashing into the net, and the home side might have won the match if it hadn't been for some alert keeping from Mearns.

The match ended all square at 1-1, both teams having played their part in an entertaining match that could have gone either way. The replay would take place four days later and with such a strong home record Barnsley would start as big favourites to progress.

Jack Cox was the Blackpool player-manager. He played for the club between 1897-98, making seventeen appearances before moving to Liverpool where he was a regular on both the left and right wing until 1909, helping them to secure their first two championships in 1901 and 1908, a period in which he also played three times for England. Cox returned to Blackpool in 1909, effectively as player-manager succeeding the club's secretary Tom Barcroft.

Blackpool: Fiske, Goulding, Whittingham, Threlfall, Connor, Clarke, Hoad, Miller, Beare, Wolstenholme, Dawson

Barnsley: Mearns, Downs, Ness, Glendenning, Boyle, Utley, Bartrop, Gadsby, Lillycrop, Tufnell, Forman

4 FA Cup First Round Replay

Thursday 20 January 1910: Oakwell, Barnsley

Barnsley   6   (Boyle, Gadsby, Lillycrop 2, Tufnell 2)
Blackpool   0
Attendance: 13,939

A Barnsley side unchanged from the first match proved much too strong for their opponents who had been forced into making one change, with Goulding still suffering from concussion being replaced by Charlie Gladwin at full back. The Seasiders were dealt a further blow within 15 minutes of the start of the game when Miller at inside-right suffered an injury to his jaw that forced him from the field for the remaining 75 minutes of match. Having been under pressure from the off, with Fiske making two decent saves, any Blackpool followers who might have made it over to Oakwell on a Thursday afternoon must have feared the worst. It was always going to be difficult with a full complement of men against a Barnsley side with seven consecutive home league victories under their belts. With a man fewer the away side's task was nigh on impossible.

It got worse when Sam Whittingham inexplicably handled the ball in his own area within minutes of Walter Miller's loss, Boyle driving the resulting penalty past the despairing dive of Fiske. Bartrop then thought he'd made it two only for the linesman to signal for offside against one of his fellow forwards, but the home side were now in total control and Gadsby soon added to the lead after a magnificent Lillycrop pass presented him with a virtually open net into which to shoot.

Lillycrop then got the goal his first-half performance merited when just before the interval he diverted Forman's centre past Fiske to make it Barnsley 3 Blackpool 0.

Perhaps it was the certainty of their success but for the first 20 minutes of the second period Barnsley rarely threatened to add to their total, but on 65 minutes Lillycrop scored his second, smashing home a centre from Forman into the far corner of the net. Tufnell scored the fifth after Fiske had done superbly to push Forman's shot for a corner. Minutes before the end it became six when Tufnell was quickest to a loose ball after Fiske had dived full length to block a Forman shot. The Blackpool keeper may have left the pitch having conceded six goals but had still performed with honour, and the defeat would have been far greater if he had allowed his head to fall.

The match had been played on a difficult muddy pitch and it was to Barnsley's credit that they had constantly played the ball out to their wingmen. Boyle in particular had grabbed the attention of the *Telegraph's* reporter for his measured passing, who also had a warning to future FA Cup opponents: 'Barnsley have become, almost imperceptibly, one of the most dangerous Cup-fighting teams in the country.'

There were 13,939 spectators at the match, considerably higher than could normally have been anticipated for an afternoon kick-off on a Thursday, when most people would have been at work. The boost to the gate was the result of the holiday that accompanied the General Election proceedings then taking place.

The victory for Barnsley meant they were lined up to travel south to Bristol Rovers in the second round. However, Bristol City, FA Cup finalists the previous season, had also been drawn at home to West Bromwich Albion. This was a match almost certain to attract the majority of football followers in the Bristol area. It was thus reported that the South Yorkshire club had written to the Rovers to see if they would be disposed to open negotiations with a view to the game being played at Oakwell. Either way both the *Telegraph* and *Independent* reckoned that Captain Boyle and his merry goalscorers would have too much for the Southern League side wherever the game eventually took place.

Barnsley: Mearns, Downs, Ness, Glendenning, Boyle, Utley, Bartrop, Gadsby, Lillycrop, Tufnell, Forman

Blackpool: Fiske, Gladwin, Whittingham, Threlfall, Connor, Clarke, Hoad, Miller, Beare, Wolstenholme, Dawson

5 Off the pitch: 1910 General Election

Barnsley kicked off their bid to win the 1910 FA Cup amidst a frenzy of electioneering. The Liberal Party had chosen to seek re-election after their 1909 'People's Budget' and proposals were passed in the House of Commons but rejected by a House of Lords, then dominated by the large landowners of the Conservative-Unionist opposition.

David Lloyd George, the Chancellor of the Exchequer in the Liberal government of Herbert Asquith, elected in 1906, was determined to 'lift the shadow of the workhouse from the homes of the poor' and believed the best way of doing this was to guarantee an income to people too old to work.

In 1908, Lloyd George introduced the Old Age Pensions Act to provide between 1 shilling [5p] and 5 shillings [25p] a week to anyone over seventy (between £2.85 and £14.25 in today's money).

However, paying for these measures would require government revenues to be raised by an additional £16 million, which he proposed to collect by increasing income tax on those earning over £3,000 (around £172,000 in current prices) to 1s and 2d (6p) in the pound with a further 'supertax' of 6d (2.5p) for those earning £5,000 a year. With an increase also proposed on inheritance tax and plans for the introduction of a land tax the proposed budget was opposed by the Conservative and Unionist Party.

The Liberals, with Winston Churchill at the front of the campaign, responded by making their proposals to reduce the power of the Lords the main issue at the January 1910 General Election, and although the Unionists gained more votes the Liberals maintained power by establishing a coalition with Labour and the Irish Nationalists, and after dropping the land tax proposal the proposed Budget was subsequently accepted by the Lords.

The conflict between the Government and Lords continued throughout 1910 until the second general election in December. This again resulted in a hung parliament with the Liberals continuing to rely on smaller coalition parties to remain in government. And it was with these that they combined to pass the Parliament Act of 1911 that asserted the supremacy of the House of Commons over the House of Lords.

The whole affair also impacted on one of the great constitutional questions of the period - the struggle in Ireland for Home Rule. The separate Kingdoms of Great Britain and Ireland had merged on 1 January 1801 and over the following years Irish opposition to the Union was strong. By 1870 the Home Rule League sought to achieve a modest form of self-government for Ireland whilst remaining part of the United Kingdom.

After the December 1910 General Election the Nationalist Irish Parliamentary Party led by John Redmond saw its chance to achieve Home

Rule, agreeing to support the Liberal Party in return for getting an agreement that Asquith would introduce a Home Rule Bill and the third such bill was introduced on 11 April 1912 - although not until May 1914 was it to finally make it through the Commons.

In four of the nine counties that constitute the historical area known as Ulster there was considerably less support for Home Rule than in the rest of Ireland. The numerically much larger Protestant community had no wish to share power with what it saw as its inferior Catholic neighbours and they wished to retain the link with Britain, especially in light of the fact that much of the highly profitable industrial enterprises that provided work were based on the link with the British Empire.

In January 1913, the Unionists established the Ulster Volunteer Force (UVF) with over 100,000 members determined to physically resist the Act's implementation by force of arms. Fully expecting that the British Army would be used to impose 'Dublin' or 'Rome Rule' the UVF imported thousands of rifles from Germany.

Meanwhile, on New Year's Day 1913, their leader, Sir Edward Carson MP, in the House of Commons moved an amendment to exclude all nine counties of Ulster from the Home Rule Bill. This attempt at partition was vigorously opposed by Nationalists who themselves began to take up arms for what seemed the inevitable Irish civil war. In the event the outbreak of larger hostilities across Europe in 1914 led to the suspension of the Act, postponing temporarily the division of Ireland into north and south.

In Barnsley, at the January 1910 Election, Joseph Walton of the Liberal Party was re-elected with a record majority of 7,372. He had first become an MP in 1897 when the previous incumbent Earl Compton became Lord Northampton and entered the House of Lords. By the time of the December 1910 election he had become Sir Joseph Walton and went on to serve as Barnsley's MP until 1922 when John Samuel Potts of the Labour Party was elected.

6 FA Cup Second Round v Bristol Rovers

Saturday 5 February 1910: Oakwell, Barnsley

Barnsley   4   (Bartrop, Gadsby, Forman, Utley)
Bristol Rovers 0

Attendance: 10,285 Receipts: £593

Bristol Rovers consolation for losing out to a fine Barnsley side came from the £500 fee they received for agreeing to swap this second round tie from their home ground to Oakwell.

Despite the Barnsley directors' decision to charge double the normal entry fee, they had still hoped to attract a crowd of close to 20,000 so the attendance of 10,285 was something of a disappointment, leaving just £93 from the total of £593 taken at the gate to pay the players and cover expenses. Consolation could be found in the team's impressive performance that took the club into the last sixteen of what was even then the most famous cup competition in the world.

Before the match the local band of the Territorial Army entertained the crowd, some of whom had travelled by special trains from Sheffield, and there was a good atmosphere when the match got under way after Boyle won the toss and set the visitors to face the breeze and a powerful sun.

The game itself stuttered into life with neither side having a shot before Barnsley struck on 12 minutes, working an opening down the left for Forman to leave McKenzie trailing in his wake. Looking up the left-winger pulled the ball back to Bartrop who in a flash hammered the ball home. This seemed to break the ice and with the Barnsley half-backs of Glendenning, Boyle and Utley dominating possession Bristol were pressed further and further back.

Lillycrop, showing his customary skill, almost made it two after he worked himself into a shooting opportunity before firing narrowly wide. Peter Roney in the Rovers goal then kept his side in the match by making a great save from a low, deadly drive from Tufnell. However, after 25 minutes, Barnsley struck for the second time, as all five forwards advanced on the Rovers' defence leaving Lillycrop to slip a ball inside to Gadsby who produced a shot of such pace that few keepers could possibly have prevented the goal.

It was now a case of how many Barnsley would score. Six had been scored at Oakwell in the 1st round replay and there was a real chance of at least as many this time such was the obvious superiority of the team in red and white. Lillycrop, playing a marvellous match, was desperately unlucky when his shot cannoned off the crossbar and away to safety. Boyle then somehow conspired to miss the goal when presented with a simple chance from only a few yards out.

Forman then found himself denied by Roney, but just on the interval the winger got his reward when after a clever dribble to take him round a couple of defenders he converged on the goalmouth before hitting a shot that struck the underside of the crossbar before entering the net. The half-time whistle sounded with the score as Barnsley 3 Bristol Rovers 0, the crowd having seen three extremely good goals.

Rovers, no doubt hoping to use the breeze to their advantage, were out first after the interval and from the start pressed forward. However, all this was to prove was the strength of the Barnsley defence, as try as they might Bristol could not even manage to fashion an opening to trouble Cooper in the home goal.

When the ball was played up to the Barnsley forwards Gadsby and Bartrop might have added to the home side's total. Finally Cooper had his most serious moment being forced to tip over the bar McColl's clever header. The keeper was then down smartly to keep out a long shot from Louis Williams as for the first time the Barnsley defence looked like they may be breached.

The arrival of the fourth goal for Barnsley finally quelled any resistance from Rovers. It came after Bartrop's cross was not fully cleared and Utley following up hit a shot that Roney could only admire as it rocketed into the net.

The *Independent* reporter at the match singled out Forman for particular praise, noting his speed and calculated centres. For the well-beaten Rovers there was special praise for the keeper Roney and his backs in front of him for sticking to their task.

Barnsley's increasingly impressive home form in league and cup would mean that few sides would welcome being drawn to play against them at Oakwell in the third round. Supporters of the club thus naturally hoped to see a home tie in the next round and they were rewarded with one when Monday's draw meant they would play the winners of the Bristol City/WBA tie that was set for a replay after finishing 1-1.

Barnsley: Cooper, Downs, Ness, Glendenning, Boyle, Utley, Bartrop, Gadsby, Lillycrop, Tufnell, Forman

Bristol Rovers: Roney, Ovens, McKenzie, Williams, Shaw, Handley, Peplow, McColl, Mason, Roberts, Lawrie

7 Off the Pitch: Dr Crippen

Hawley Harvey Crippen was an American, born in Michigan in 1862, who qualified as a doctor in 1885 and worked for a patent medicine company. He had come to England in 1900 and lived at 39 Hilldrop Crescent, Holloway with his second wife Cora Turner, who was better known by her stage name of Belle Elmore.

After a party at their home on 31 January 1910 Cora disappeared and shortly afterwards Crippen moved his mistress Ethel le Neve into the house, and she began to wear his wife's clothing and jewelry. Cora Turner's friends reported their suspicions to the police. Crippen had been telling people that she had moved back to the USA to see a sick relative. Detective Chief Inspector Walter Dew visited Crippen, and left the premises after Crippen had claimed that his wife had eloped with a lover, and a search had not revealed anything of a suspicious nature.

Dew's visit panicked Crippen and Ethel le Neve into leaving the country for Antwerp, from where they took a cabin on SS *Montrose* bound for Canada. Alerted by their disappearance Scotland Yard performed another three searches of the house and during the fourth and final one remains of a human body were discovered beneath the cellar. Dr Bernard Spilsbury, the famous pathologist, identified the body as that of Mrs Crippen from a piece of abdominal scar tissue, and found that there were traces of a poison, hyoscine, in the body.

The search for Crippen was assisted by the Master of the SS *Montrose*. He suspected that the 'boy' accompanying one of his passengers, Mr Robinson, was Ethel le Neve in disguise. He entered history by the first use of the telegraph to relay his conclusions to the ship's owners and the police. Walter Dew took a faster ship, the SS *Laurentic*, and arrested Crippen on 31 July before he could land in Canada.

At Crippen's trial the jury took just 27 minutes to convict him of murder and John Ellis hanged him on 23 November 1910, at Pentonville Prison, London. Ethel le Neve was acquitted. In 1962 a feature film, Dr Crippen, featured Donald Pleasance in the title role.

8 FA Cup Third Round v West Bromwich Albion

Saturday 19 February 1910: Oakwell, Barnsley
Barnsley	1	(Tufnell, 80 minutes)
West Bromwich Albion	0	
Attendance:	18,636	

JJ Bentley writing in the *Daily Express*:

> This should prove a rousing tie, with the odds slightly in favour of Barnsley who are a very difficult side to beat on their own ground which by the way is not nearly as bad as many people appear to think. It is, at any rate, much better than it was a few years ago...I should imagine this will be one of the hardest ties in the whole round, full of vigour and fire.

With West Brom beating Bristol City 4-2 at the Hawthorns in the second round replay there was little doubt that the attraction of such prestigious opponents

**Captain Tommy Boyle prior to winning the toss before the start of the 3rd round
FA Cup tie with West Bromwich Albion. Looking on are his opposite number
Jessie Pennington, Mr Adams (referee) and a record Oakwell crowd of 18,836.
Bower Collection**

in the last sixteen of the Cup would attract a record Oakwell crowd.

West Brom were certain to prove doughty cup fighters, having won the competition on two previous occasions. Firstly in 1888, the season before the Football League was born, 'the Baggies' beat near neighbours Wednesday Old Athletic, Birmingham Saint George's and Wolverhampton Wanderers, before enjoying a bye in round four en route to beating Stoke City, Old Carthusians and Derby Junction to set up a encounter in the final with Preston North End in a match played at the Kennington Oval.

Nineteen thousand spectators witnessed a fine encounter with Jimmy Bayliss earning WBA a half-time lead with a goal after eight minutes. Fred Dewhurst equalised soon after the restart but West Brom were not to be denied and 13 minutes from the end George Woodall scored what proved to be the winner. It was a case of third time lucky for the Black Country side after having suffered the disappointment of losing to Blackburn Rovers and Aston Villa in the previous two finals.

West Brom gained revenge for the latter result by beating Villa in the 1891-92 final with goals from Jasper Geddes, Sam Nicholls and Jack Reynolds but three years later when the sides met for the third (and to date final time) Villa reversed the reverse by winning 1-0 at Crystal Palace.

Barnsley and West Brom had met earlier in the season in a game played at the Hawthorns, with the home side winning a thrilling encounter 4-3. The sides were neck and neck in the league, both on 25 points, with West Brom having played a game more. The away side arrived at Oakwell having recorded more away victories in Division II than any side and had of course grabbed a draw at First Division Bristol City in the previous round. Yet such was Barnsley's home form, with twelve victories and one draw from the last thirteen league and cup games at Oakwell, then it was clear that if West Brom were to still entertain hopes of a third cup success at the end of the 90 minutes then they would have to play exceptionally well.

The match was to be played in windy conditions broken by squally showers. Despite heavy rain throughout the week the *Independent's* 'Ranger' felt that 'the ground was in a very fair condition' for the 18,836 spectators, which was as anticipated a record Oakwell attendance.

Having won the toss, Boyle wasted no time in deciding to force West Brom, with the 'Spion Kop' at their backs, to open the game kicking against the wind and they also had the sun to face at intervals when it deigned to make a welcome appearance.

A corner: action from the Barnsley v West Brom cup-tie, 19 February 1910. Bower Collection

Within two minutes of the start Hubert Pearson was forced to make a smart save from Tufnell. The keeper was not troubled however by shots from Gadsby and Lillycrop, the wind taking the ball well wide on both occasions.

With Harry Burton and Jesse Pennington quick to snuff out any danger West Brom were coping comfortably enough at the back to venture forward themselves and Fred Buck with a tremendous drive was unfortunate when the ball rocketed back off the crossbar with Cooper well beaten. Charlie Hewitt should have done better just minutes later but with only the keeper to beat he rolled his shot wide of the post.

Bartrop then threatened to open up the West Brom defence but on the occasions when he was able to pull back the ball across the penalty area the Barnsley forwards were nowhere to be seen. So when the whistle sounded for half-time at 0-0 there must have been a number of home supporters who felt that the failure to score with the wind did not bode well for their side in the second period. (*The Ranger* and *Barnsley Chronicle* reporters both felt, in their match reports, that Barnsley's chance had gone at half-time)

Yet they need not have worried as Barnsley started the second half in good fashion, getting the ball down and playing it around with confidence, Bartrop forcing Pearson to grab the ball from just under the bar. Bob Pailor could have opened the scoring just after but his header flashed past the post with Cooper absent. Then on 65 minutes Forman made a great run to leave the West Brom defenders trailing in this wake before delivering a perfectly weighted pass but sadly Tufnell failed to hit the ball cleanly and it passed across the goal with Bartrop diving desperately to get a touch as it flashed out for a goal kick.

With the pitch starting to churn up, the reporter for the *Barnsley Chronicle* noted that a number of the players were finding it difficult to keep up with the pace of the game which with each passing minute seemed destined to end up with a replay at the Hawthorns. Barnsley certainly couldn't afford that, not with a record of just one away win all season - it was a case of surely now or never.

As the match entered the final quarter it became even more keenly contested, and although it was never a classic the crowd were enthralled and those in red and white urged the Barnsley players to get forward. When Downs was forced to retire from the pitch that seemed certain to ensure West Brom would live to fight another day and so there was a big cheer when he ran back out from underneath the stands after an absence of around five minutes.

It was the little right back who played an important part in the winning goal after 80 minutes, dribbling forward before finding Lillycrop who beat a couple of defenders before passing to Tufnell whose lovely cross shot gave Pearson no chance. 1-0 to Barnsley.

Firth Collection

Try as they might after that West Brom never really looked like scoring and when referee A Adams from Nottingham sounded the final whistle Barnsley had made it through to the quarter-finals of the FA Cup for the second time in their history.

According to the *Barnsley Chronicle*, 'Downs played a champion game' but the halves in Glendenning, Boyle and Utley had been the stars of the show in a game of few real chances. Pearson was rated as West Bromwich Albion's best player but there was also praise for Barton and Frank Waterhouse. It had been a difficult game but one that Barnsley just about deserved to win.

Barnsley: Cooper, Downs, Ness, Glendenning, Boyle, Utley, Bartrop, Gadsby, Lillycrop, Tufnell, Forman

WBA: Pearson, Burton, Pennington, Garraty, Waterhouse, Manners, Hewitt, Bowser, Pailor, Bucks, Simpson

The draw on the Monday brought the exciting news that Barnsley would be at home in the quarter-finals to either Queens Park Rangers (QPR) or West Ham United who were to replay after drawing 1-1 in the first match at the Park Royal Ground. (QPR didn't move to Loftus Road until 1917.)

'Yorkshire's Hope': Barnsley's 1910 Cup team, from a G W Irving compilation.
Bower Collection

9 Players' wages in 1910

Players in 1910 were very badly treated by their employers. The maximum wage had been introduced in 1901 preventing them earning more than £4 a week until 1909 when it was increased to £5 (about £285 today). They were also restricted from moving to another club under the 'retain and transfer' system that then operated. Under this, clubs could keep a player until they wanted to transfer him. With injured players forced out of the game unable to expect any compensation it was hardly surprising that the players had got together to form the Players' Union and Benefit Society at a meeting in Manchester on 2 December 1907.

However, it was to be a long struggle, one which lasted over half a century before the players, under the able leadership of Jimmy Hill and later Derek Dougan smashed both the maximum wage and the retain and transfer system, the downside of which has been to ensure that the better supported and financed sides can lure away their opponents better players, thus reducing the chances of teams like Barnsley ever repeating their successes of 1910 and 1912.

10 FA Cup Fourth Round v Queen's Park Rangers

Saturday 5 March 1910: Oakwell, Barnsley

Barnsley	1	(Bartrop)
QPR	0	
Attendance:	23,574	

By beating Queen's Park Rangers Barnsley qualified for their first ever appearance in the FA Cup semi-final. The match was watched by a then record Oakwell crowd of 24,000 who were afterwards joined by thousands more on the town's streets all keen to discuss whether the club could make it to the final at Crystal Palace.

Possible semi-final opponents in Monday afternoon's draw were the all-conquering Newcastle United, reigning First Division Champions, and Everton, FA Cup winners in 1906. Everyone agreed the side they hoped to see as the next round opponents were Swindon Town of the Southern League, who'd beaten Manchester City in the quarter-finals.

Captain Tommy Boyle (right) at the start of the kick-off , Barnsley v Queens Park Rangers, 4th round of the FA Cup, 5 March 1910. Bower Collection

The numbers at the match would have been considerably more if room on the terraces could have been found to accommodate them, but half an hour before kick-off it was necessary to close the gates. Amongst the crowd were 400 Rangers followers described in the *Independent* as 'making a brave show with their neat green and white badges'.

The match itself was not a glorious affair with the importance of the occasion appearing to affect a number of the players, the game being the biggest some of them had played so far in their careers.

Barnsley's front five with a dry ground and little wind to trouble them were for much of the match easily held by the Rangers' defence. However, any hopes the Londoners had of building on this solid platform were snuffed out by the hard- working Barnsley defence in which Downs, at right-back, and Boyle at centre-half were outstanding, the latter dominating Bill Steer, the scorer of five FA Cup goals in the previous three rounds for QPR.

Centre-halves back in 1910 however were not simply content to block out the opposing centre forward and indeed up until 1925 and a change in the offside law, reducing the numbers behind the last attacking player from three to two for an offside, they had been attacking players around which much of the play was directed. Dashing forward, Boyle was able to beat his opposing QPR centre-half Ambrose Hartwell with relative ease to hammer a number of shots that Frank Shaw in goal did well to prevent entering the net.

The keeper might have done better after 25 minutes when QPR conceded the only goal of the match. It came when, following a brave determined run forward, left back Ness found Gadsby whose pass was collected by Bartrop. Glancing up the outside-right aimed his cross at the heads of the on-rushing Tufnell and Lillycrop in the middle and when Shaw rushed from his line to block the danger he was left in no-man's land after the wind took the ball over him to end up in the net after first hitting the far post. It may have been a fortunate goal but that didn't stop the Barnsley players rushing over to overwhelm the scorer with their congratulations.

Stung by going behind, QPR roared forward but Barnsley's defence stood strong to ensure the score remained 1-0 at half time.

The match should have been over shortly after the restart when a lovely centre from Forman needed only a push home from Bartrop to make it two, a heavy touch sadly sending the ball over the bar with an empty net gaping.

Towards the end, the game became a scrappy affair and with nothing to lose both of QPR's full-backs, John Macdonald and Joe Fiddler, and Ambrose Hartwell piled forward determined to support their forwards' efforts to grab the equaliser. Their task was not helped when Steer was carried off with a fractured rib after a clash with Downs, reducing the away side to ten men. Yet

Will Bartrop (not in view) scores the winning goal v QPR, 5 March 1910.
Bower Collection

it is likely that even with twelve men QPR could not have hoped to get past the outstanding Boyle, whom both the *Independent*, describing him as a prospective England international, and *Telegraph* warmly praised.

The end of the game brought with it the most tumultuous scenes Oakwell had ever experienced with the large crowd cheering the victorious XI to the dressing rooms and then, according to the *Independent*, heading off to 'swamp the refreshment houses and swoop down upon anything in the form of food, such that it may have dawned on some trades people at last that there is a commercial side to football enterprise which is worthy of encouragement'.

Receipts for the match were £780, which were less than when Barnsley played Woolwich Arsenal at the same stage of the competition in 1906-07 when the club directors' decision to charge a shilling (5p) entry fee had boosted the gate income at the expense of a crowd which was little more than half the size of that which watched the 1910 quarter-final.

Firth Collection

Barnsley: Mearns, Downs, Ness, Glendenning, Boyle, Utley, Bartrop, Gadsby, Lillycrop, Tufnell, Forman

QPR: Shaw, Macdonald, Fiddler, Mitchell, Hartwell, Wake, McNaught, Travers, W. Steer*, Whyman, Barnes

* It was customary in match reports to give amateur players in a side the honour of their initial, professionalism being still somewhat frowned up even after many years in which the majority of players were paid for their craft.

The QPR manager James Cowan had been appointed as the club's first official manager in 1907, leading his side to the Southern League title in his first season. Cowan played for Aston Villa from 1887 to 1902, winning five First Division and two FA Cup winners medals. In all he played 354 times for Villa and is considered to be one of the finest footballers of the Victorian era. Cowan was also a Scottish international. Although he was a half-back he was also extremely quick, winning the then illustrious 100-yard 'New Year Sprint' event held at Powderhall in Glasgow and the prize money that went with it.

ocal photographer Will Randall's amusing interpretation clearly shows Barnsley were still in the FA Cup. Bower Collection

'The triumphant rise of Barnsley', in the 1910 FA Cup, as illustrated by G W Irving. Note the shot of Oakwell showing the Spion Kop and brewery side. Bower Collection

This comic Randall card also includes a funny reference to 'Amos', the club mascot whose shirt carries the legend 'Yorkshire's Last Hope'. Bower Collection

Another witty Irving postcard, from 1910, 'campaigning' for a 'monument' in praise of Barnsley FC's cup success. Bower Collection

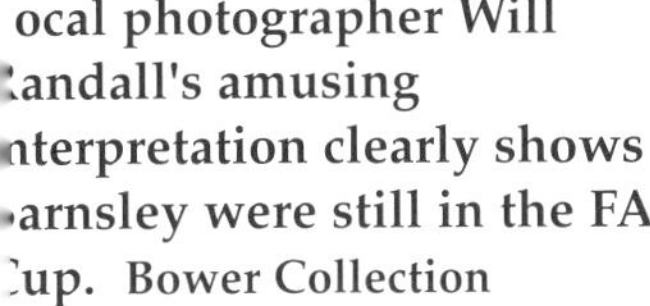

11 FA Cup Semi-Final v Everton

Saturday 26 March 1910: Elland Road, Leeds

Barnsley   0
Everton   0
Attendance: 35,000

With only one defeat in twelve matches Everton, as the First Division team and FA Cup winners in 1905-06 were favourites with the bookmakers to win through to their fifth FA Cup Final. Betting on football matches is almost as old as the FA Cup itself as the first reference to betting on the outcome of football matches appears to be that Royal Engineers were installed as 4/7 favourites to win the first FA Cup Final in 1872 – they lost.

Within five years betting on several matches taking place on the same day appears to have already been established. Not everyone was happy with this state of affairs with the *Birmingham Guardian* declaring it was a 'nuisance' as it had led many men to wager their week's wages on the outcome of the 1887 final between Aston Villa and WBA. For years the football authorities were to maintain a strict policy of non-engagement with bookmakers and the gambling industry.

Despite their Second Division status, Barnsley were confident of causing an upset and thousands of their followers joined those from Merseyside and neutral observers in packing out the ground such that the gates had to be closed one and a half hours before kick-off with a crowd of 33,000 paying just under £2,500 for the privilege of seeing the great occasion.

When Bartrop threatened to make an early breakthrough Jock Maconnachie cleared confidently. Boyle at the Barnsley back was finding Bertie Freeman a real handful and the tussle proved one of the game's many highlights.

Barnsley supporters thought their side had taken the lead when Lillycrop's header from a wonderful Bartrop cross looked set to drop into the Everton goal only for Val Harris to head the ball up and over the bar for a corner. When Boyle was left shaken by a rough challenge the Yorkshire side were grateful to a timely interception by Ness to prevent Freeman dashing into the clear. The Everton man was unfortunate later on in the half when Mearns produced a sprawling save to deny him at the cost of a heavy blow, which left the keeper needing attention.

The match remained goalless at half-time but the deadlock should have been broken just after the restart only for Lillycrop to put the ball the wrong side of the post with only the keeper to beat. By now Barnsley were controlling the game, but they failed to make use of their numerous corners and although

George Washington Irving also produced several comic/dialect cards, including this one, teasing the 'toffee men' of Everton. Bower Collection

Forman was able to get to the by-line with ease his crossing was poor leaving his fellow forwards frustrated. With the pressure building it looked only a matter of time before the Second Division side took the lead. Perhaps realising just how close they were to making it to THE FA CUP FINAL the normally reliable Barnsley forwards couldn't hammer home the blow of the decisive goal as the Everton backs, including Harry Makepeace were left to fight another day with the game ending 0-0.

Makepeace is unique in the world of sport as he is the only man to win an FA Cup and League Championship winner's medal (both with Everton), be capped as a soccer international (with England four times), win a County Cricket Championship medal (with Lancashire on four occasions) and be capped as a cricket international (four England caps versus Australia in 1920/21). What odds would you get with the bookmakers for anyone doing that nowadays?

Barnsley: Mearns, Downs, Ness, Glendenning, Boyle, Utley, Bartrop, Gadsby, Lillycrop, Tufnell, Forman

Everton: Scott, Clifford, McConnachie, Harris, Taylor, Makepeace, Sharpe, White, Freeman, Young, Barlow

12 FA Cup Semi-Final Replay v Everton

Thursday 31st March 1910: Old Trafford, Manchester

Barnsley   3   (Gadsby, Forman, Tufnell)
Everton   0
Attendance: 55,000

To the utter jubilation of their ecstatic supporters Barnsley made it through to their first FA Cup Final with a wonderful performance that gave Everton no chance. The match was the first of many subsequent thrillers on, Wembley aside, Britain's best-known ground, Old Trafford, that had first opened its doors just a few weeks earlier when Manchester United played Liverpool there in early February.

In 1908, Second Division Wolves had shocked the football world by beating First Division giants Newcastle United, now Second Division Barnsley would have the chance to do the same with the Geordies having beaten Swindon Town 2-0 in the other semi-final.

The result showed that the Barnsley side were very different from the one that had gone down disappointingly in the previous seasons FA Cup 1st round

The kick-off, Barnsley v Everton semi-final replay at Old Trafford, Tommy Boyle on the left. Bower Collection

when Everton had knocked them out by winning 3-1. And it also knocked for six critics who had attributed the Tykes' success to the peculiarities of their Oakwell ground and pitch, as any team who knock home sixteen goals against just one in seven matches to win through to the FA Cup final must be 'a good 'un'.

Everton, it has to be said, were unfortunate on the day, being forced due to injuries to play 75 minutes of the game with ten men and even on occasions with just nine. Yet Barnsley, having had the better of the first game, were confident and expectation was high and their followers in the 55,000 crowd, 19,000 more than at Elland Road, were in great heart before kick-off.

After 15 minutes in which Everton had enjoyed more possession the game was held up for some time when centre-half Jack Taylor the Everton captain was struck in the neck by a fierce shot which fractured his larynx and compelled him to retire from the game. The injury in fact proved so serious that it effectively ended Taylor's professional career in which he had played in three FA Cup finals in 1897, 1906 and 1907, the first as a right-winger and the latter ones as a centre-half. Taylor is currently one of only six players to have made 400 Football League appearances for Everton.

The injury forced a reshuffle to the Merseysiders' team, White being withdrawn to the half-back line-up, reducing the forwards to four who rarely

Harry Tufnell scoring the third goal during the Barnsley v Everton FA Cup Semi-final at Old Trafford, Manchester, 31 March 1910. Firth Collection

threatened after that to knock the ball past Mearns in the Barnsley goal. Despite their one-man advantage it took some time for Barnsley to exploit it with only Bartrop threatening Billy Scott in the Everton goal. Irishman Scott played twenty-five times for his country between 1903 and 1913, and was a member of the famous Ireland team that beat England for the first time with a 2-1 win at Windsor Park.

The South Yorkshire side were given a marvellous opportunity to take the lead just after the half hour mark when Harris handled. Sadly Boyle put the penalty kick well wide. Everton were then given a similar opportunity to go in front after Glendenning charged over Alex 'Sandy' Young, scorer of the 1906 FA Cup final winning goal and First Division top goal scorer in 1906-07. Young's death in 1959 continues to remain something of a mystery as according to reports he was either hanged for sheep rustling in Australia or died in an Edinburgh asylum. Young's memory is still celebrated at Goodison Park in the shape of a historic mosaic hanging from one of the walls inside the ground.

Sharp hit his shot well but straight at Mearns who managed to gather and as a consequence the match remained goalless at half-time. It did not remain that way long as on 50 minutes Barnsley took the lead.

The goal came when Forman attacked down the left, eluded Bob Clifford and shot at close range. Scott, making a valiant effort, hurled himself to block

Firth Collection

and in the almighty scrimmage that followed Gadsby belted home to make it 1-0. Scott, having had his hand trodden on, was forced from the field and for the next ten minutes nine-man Everton had McConnachie between the posts and he made a fine save from Lillycrop before Scott came back to take over in goal.

Everton had an opportunity to equalise when Freeman slipped his way past the two Barnsley full-backs and, after beating Mearns, seemed certain to score, only to push his shot wide of the empty goal from ten yards out.

With just five minutes remaining Barnsley ended the contest with their second goal, Gadsby running clear of Clifford, found Forman who finished in style. Scarcely had the game restarted when Lillycrop dribbled his way through the tired Everton defence and pushed the ball into the running path of Tufnell who crashed home.

When the referee brought proceedings to a halt Barnsley had thus recorded the most famous victory in their twenty-three-year history. Grit, determination, speed and a touch of good fortune on the day had all played their part.

Barnsley: Mearns, Downs, Ness, Glendenning, Boyle, Utley, Bartrop, Gadsby, Lillycrop, Tufnell, Forman

Everton: Scott, Clifford, McConnachie, Harris, Taylor, Makepeace, Sharpe, White, Freeman, Young, Barlow

With the Cup Final still more than three weeks away, Barnsley had a number of league games to play before the big day, and more than 10,000 passed through the Oakwell turnstiles for only the second time in the league for the game with Manchester City on 2 April, Gadsby scoring in a 1-1 draw. This was followed by defeats away at Clapton Orient and Leicester Fosse, before a victory at home to WBA 2-1 and a 2-1 defeat at Lincoln City the weekend before the Cup Final with Newcastle. The Geordies' form had been better with a win and two draws in their four games between their semi-final success and the final.

13 Newcastle United: Cup Final Opponents

Barnsley's FA Cup final opponents were Newcastle United of the First Division. The Geordies had beaten Stoke, after a replay, Fulham, Blackburn Rovers, Leicester Fosse and finally Swindon Town in the semi-final to make it to Crystal Palace. Newcastle had won the First Division title in three of the five

Barnsley's team portrayed as 'The Yorkshire Rose' for the FA Cup Final v Newcastle United. Bower Collection

Will Randall's imaginative image of of Barnsley's 1910 Cup Final team, showing the latest form of transport – the aeroplane. Bower Collection

previous seasons, including in 1908-09. The contest seemed a formality in light of the fact that Barnsley had not even come anywhere near getting promoted to Division 1 never mind winning it. Yet the side from St James' Park had been in this position just two years previously, only in 1908 it was mid-table Wolverhampton Wanderers who barred their way to a first FA Cup success. Having previously lost to Aston Villa in the 1905 final and Everton twelve months later no-one expected a side led by Colin Veitch to falter a third time. This however was exactly what happened, Wolves winning 3-1, a match which witnessed the last ever amateur to score a goal in the final, the Reverend Kenneth Hunt opening the scoring for the winning side in the 40th minute.

There was also disquiet in the Newcastle dressing room in the lead-up to the game. Firstly, after a tame match at Ayresome Park ended with Middlesbrough gaining the point they needed to stave off relegation the referee, Alan Green of Birmingham, reported both clubs to the Football League for what he considered to have been the rigging of the game. Although a commission later cleared both clubs the incident must have done little for morale. Much more important was the incident in which Newcastle's star centre-forward Albert Shepherd was accused of having been 'got at' only days before the semi-final with Swindon Town. When he was subsequently left out of the cup squad his colleagues were left bewildered, and it was only after they demanded his return for the final that the directors were forced to play him or risk having a strike on their hands.

Barnsley therefore had every right to fancy their chances and as the report later on the first game shows they could easily have sent Newcastle back as defeated cup finalists once again.

14 Newcastle Player-Profiles

Jimmy Lawrence – still holds the record for the most Newcastle first team appearances with 496 in a career lasting from 1904 to 1922. A goalkeeper who preferred to fist the ball away Lawrence could also pull of a stunning save but had played poorly in the 1905 final when Newcastle had gone down 2-0 to Aston Villa, consolation for which came in the form of a first of three league title wins in five seasons during which he was a first team regular.

Bill McCracken – Belfast-born McCracken was one of the best but also one of most loathed footballers of his generation. This was as a result of his mastery of the off-side trap, which when it was introduced in 1866 meant a player could be off-side if there were fewer than three players between him and the opposing goal line when the ball was played. Full-back McCracken, one of the game's thinkers, realised that a more effective way of stopping attacks than dispossessing the forwards was to move craftily up field at opportune times and catch them offside. McCracken so organised his defence that forwards were regularly caught offside. Although his tactics were seen as effective they were also viewed as unsporting and angered many opposing players and spectators.

The laws were changed in 1925, two years after McCracken retired at the end of a nineteen-year playing career with Newcastle in which he collected three League and one FA Cup winner's medals and made well over 400 first team appearances. McCracken also represented Ireland and, following the partition of the country in 1921, Northern Ireland on fifteen occasions, scoring a single goal.

Tony Whiston – a tough, durable full-back who had become a first team regular during the 1908-09 title winning season. Described by Paul Joannou in *Black N' White Alphabet* as an 'accurate distributor of the ball who was well remembered for a well-timed sliding tackle.' Whiston made 146 first team appearances in total for Newcastle.

Colin Veitch – Newcastle-born Veitch made his debut at nineteen before becoming a regular in the 1902-03 season. Generally regarded as a midfield player, he was also versatile enough to play in most other positions during his long career in a period when for much of the time Newcastle were England's number one side. Veitch was a leading figure in the Association Football Players Union (AFPU) at a time when players were badly exploited, serving as the chairman until he retired from football on the outbreak of the First World War. It is likely that Veitch would have won more than six caps for his country if it wasn't for his role in the Union as he was an astute reader of the game and a natural captain on and off the field. These qualities, combined with his versatility, would win him a place in any best ever Newcastle line-up. Veitch was also a close friend of playwright George Bernard Shaw and a committed socialist.

Wilf Low – had moved from Aberdeen to Newcastle in the summer of 1909 and in a career broken by the war went on to make 378 first team appearances before later becoming the trainer at St James' Park. A big strapping centre-half who operated in midfield to destroy the opposition's attacking moves including those of his brother's side, Sunderland. Also earned five Scottish international caps during his period in England. Low's cousin, William, played forty-two games for Barnsley between 1920 and 1922.

Peter McWilliam – played close to 250 games for Newcastle at left-half between 1902 and 1911 during which time he earned the crowd's title of 'Peter the Great' and won three league championship medals. A great passer of the ball, McWilliam possessed the ability to swerve past his opponents and made eight appearances for Scotland in a career shortened by injury. After the war he managed Spurs to the Second Division title and when the London side won the FA Cup in 1921 McWilliam thus became the first man to win the competition as a player and as a manager.

Jock Rutherford – a local lad who would have been an outstanding forward in any era. Scorer of ninety-four goals from outside-right in 336 first team appearances with Newcastle from 1902 until an argument over his benefit money took him south to play for Woolwich Arsenal. Style, speed and control, added to his remarkable consistency made him a firm crowd favourite and helped him to win eleven England caps.

James Howie – another Scot who joined Newcastle in May 1903 and ended up winning three league winner's medals. Howie formed a deadly partnership down the right with Rutherford, utilising his remarkable dribbling skills and eye for a goal that saw him score eighty-two times in 237 appearances to perfection. Had scored three times during Newcastle's run to the 1910 FA Cup final.

Albert Shepherd – rated by Charlie Buchan, the Sunderland, Arsenal and England legend, as the best centre-forward in English football prior to World War One. Extremely quick and powerful, Shepherd was the First Division top scorer in the 1905-06 season with twenty-five goals and was to amass a highly impressive ninety-two goals in 123 appearances for Newcastle. Shepherd had a lethal shot and an abiding passion for scoring goals.

Alex 'Sandy' Higgins – initially struggled to establish himself as a first team player after being signed from Kilmarnock in June 1905 but came to prominence during Newcastle's title winning 1908-09 campaign. Higgins had scored four goals in the FA Cup in 1910, but with Shepherd monopolising the centre-forward position he had been pushed to inside-left, from where he could utilise his inimitable passing skills. Higgins collected a Scottish Cup winner's medal back with Kilmarnock in 1920 but missed the final itself when his father died on the morning of the game.

Albert Shepherd, the scorer of Newcastle's goals in the 1910 FA Cup Final replay at Goodison Park, against Sunderland. Days Collection

George Wilson – cost Newcastle a then record fee of £1,600 when signed in November 1907 from Everton, where after appearing in six of the seven games leading up to the final he was dropped prior to the 1907 Cup Final after complaining about the side's style of play. Wilson became a firm favourite with the Newcastle crowd. Tricky and fast, victory against Barnsley would enable the six-time capped Scot, to join the elite band of players who have won both Scottish and English cup winner's medals.

Jack Carr – replaced Whiston in replay – a local lad who made his debut in December 1899. Originally a left-half, Carr moved to left back when McWilliam established himself in the first team, where his physical no-nonsense style not only endeared him to the fans but also helped him win two England caps. Winner of three Division 1 medals.

15 The 1910 FA Cup Final v Newcastle United

Saturday 23 April 1910: Crystal Palace Grounds, Sydenham

Barnsley	1	(Tufnell, 37min)
Newcastle United	1	(Rutherford, 83min)
Attendance:	77,747	

The following match report is taken from the *Barnsley Independent*:

STORY OF THE STRUGGLE
HOW BARNSLEY HAD THE LEAD
AND LOST IT
WELL MATCHED FOES

Barnsley have not yet won the Cup, they missed doing so on Saturday by the narrowest of margins. But their performance inspired the greater proportion of those who witnessed the keen encounter and the admirable enclosure at the Crystal Palace with confidence that they will lift the coveted trophy if they play with the same spirit and dauntless energy at Everton on Thursday.

This view is not shared only by partisans from the colliery town and its environs. There were scores of people from the north who share this belief. That Newcastle people were disappointed with the display given by the Tynesiders was clear. Like Yorkshire folk they say what they think. But, like Yorkshire people, also, they are true sportsman and if their favourites are not good enough to achieve the success they desire they are the first to applaud the side, which outplayed them.

One disappointed Novocastrian after commenting on the feebleness of the general display of a 'team of all talents' concluded with the observation 'Well, if Newcastle can't win the Cup. They ought to be given it for good attendance.'

Souvenir card published by WH Smith for the Newcastle-Barnsley final, featuring Colin Veitch. WH Smith

An artist's impression of match action from the 1910 Final at Crystal Palace. Jon Wilkinson

Bearing in mind Newcastle's previous record, all one can say is that there may be something in the Northerner's conclusion.

The crowd was a particularly happy one, and thoroughly good-natured. Not the least conspicuous were the fifty trippers who had gained the *Sheffield Independent* prizes enabling them to witness the match free. They enjoyed themselves thoroughly in every way, and according to one of them had a real royal time. They got to London in excellent time, and were to be seen during the morning busily engaged in sightseeing.

It is not surprising that the Londoners at the Palace were mostly friendly towards the Barnsley supporters. Their boisterous enthusiasm pleased them, their rich Yorkshire dialect amused them, and the unbounded confidence they displayed in their team captivated them and they cheered for Barnsley too. It was a great day for Barnsley. Thursday will be a greater day if all hopes are realised.

By 'Centre-Forward'

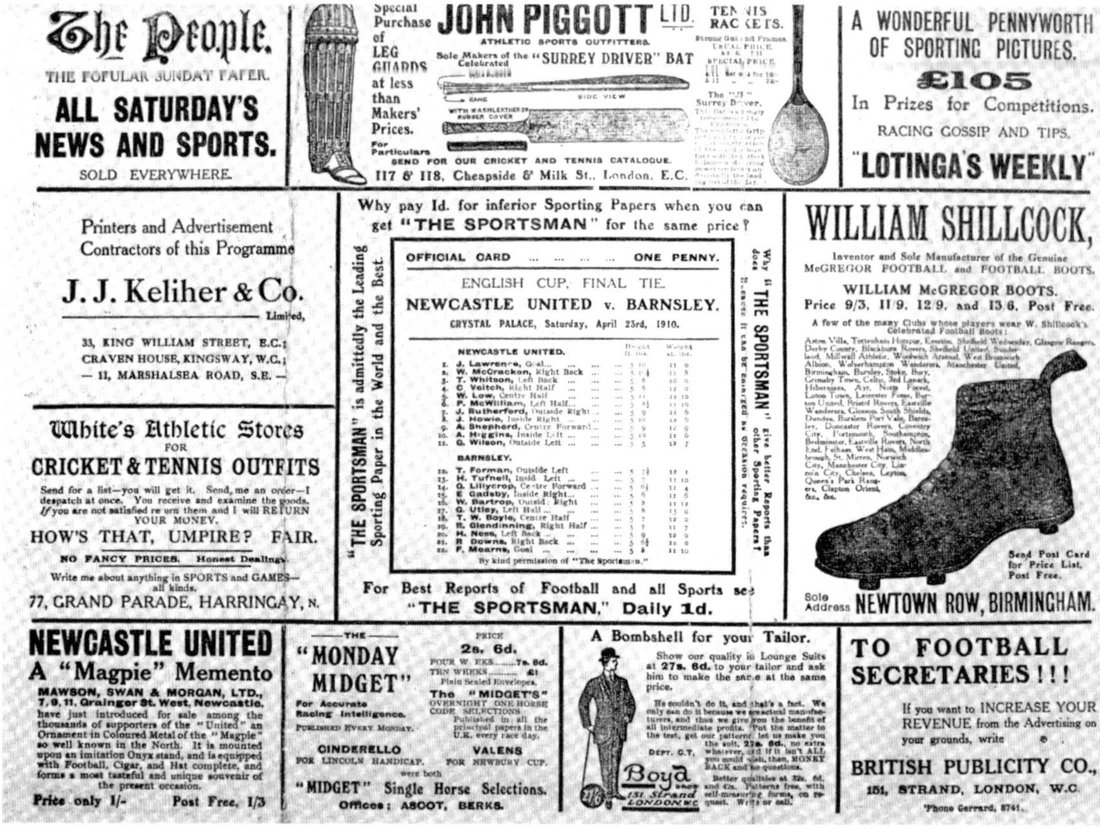

Official programme for the 1910 Newcastle v Barnsley FA Cup Final.
Wood Collection

The tens of thousands of spectators who spread themselves over the slopes of Sydenham on Saturday witnessed an English Cup final which as a display of football was little, if any, above the average seen in these great annual struggles. Somehow, the greatness of the occasion seems to prevent the contending teams giving their best form, and probably it will be a long time before we see such another great exhibition as that we were favoured three years ago, in the contest wherein Aston Villa vanquished Everton by 3 goals to 2.

So far as Saturday's conflict is concerned, the Barnsley team appeared to me to come nearer to their best form than did Newcastle, who, with the possible exception of Aston Villa, may be regarded as the most scientific combination of the season. The result of the game was to my mind a perfect vindication of the merits of the teams as shown during a sternly fought 90 minutes of vigorous and at times exciting football. They each scored one goal,

Wood Collecti

The Final that Called for a New Game : The Drawn Match at the Crystal Palace.

NEWCASTLE UNITED v. BARNSLEY: BARNSLEY'S GOALKEEPER SAVING.

The Association Football Cup Final took place at the Crystal Palace on Saturday of last week before some 80,000 spectators. The contestants were Newcastle United and Barnsley. Each team scored one goal, and it was arranged that the re-play should take place at Everton on the Thursday of this week.—[PHOTOGRAPH BY ILLUSTRATIONS BUREAU.]

This illustration was published in the *Illustrated London News* on 30 April 1910. Illustrated London News

and neither was an exactly brilliant one, and if Newcastle did the greater share of attacking, they found opposed to them a defence so powerful as to gain the chief honours of a hard fought game.

The Crowd

The Barnsley team had the heartier welcome when, following their more renowned opponents, they entered the arena, but I have known more wildly enthusiastic receptions given to other teams in other days. Doubtless the fierce partisanship of the immediate friends of each club was lost in the impartiality of an assemblage of whom the great majority had no special interest in the success

A still taken from movie footage of the 1910 FA Cup Final at Crystal Palace showing George Utley leaving the field. To mark the special occasion, the Barnsley shirts carried an embroidery of the town crest. Wood Collection

Ladies supporters' badge. Wood Collection

of either side. Expectation that the clever Novocastrians would on this occasion make amends for three previous failures mingled with admiration for the pluck and Cup-fighting grit which had carried a team in the position of Barnsley so far in the great national competition seemed to be the prevailing sentiments among hosts of Metropolitan enthusiasts, who, judging from casual remarks one heard, were as much concerned in the League fate of the Spurs and Chelsea as in the destination of the English Cup. The spectators however grew keenly interested and awoke to bursts of enthusiasm as the game progressed. Of course the numbers fell far short of the record of 110,920, which was the attendance when Sheffield United and Tottenham Hotspur played a drawn game in the final nine years ago. Such figures will probably never be equalled until another London club takes part in the struggle.

Newcastle's Vain Attack

Barnsley were represented by the same eleven who had dismissed Everton from the semi-final. The Tynesiders, in the hope of seeing him doing some of his famous sharp shooting reintroduced Shepherd into the centre forward position, but the change did not as it happened serve to strengthen the Northern attack. The Yorkshire men losing the toss had a fair breeze against them during the first half. The early stages of the struggle saw the Novocastirans persistently on the aggressive, and the first half hour's play consisted for the most part of a tussle between their forwards and the Barnsley defence, in which the latter got the best of it. The northerners did enough pressing to warrant the feeling that they would be first to score, but although their wing men often took the ball along well and centred Mearns in the Barnsley goal was given very little to do. Once Rutherford swung the ball across where Shepherd stood in a favourable position but he failed to gather it, and muffed what looked like a good opening. The best shot indeed was sent in by Colin Veitch, who from half back whizzed the ball only a few inches, the wrong side of the post with Mearns making a flying leap across at a superb shot which would have been certain to beat him.

Barnsley's Goal

All this time the defence of the Yorkshiremen had been great. A truly splendid pair of backs were Downs and Ness, and the manner in which the former got his side out of difficulties by astute tackling or clever overhead kicks especially awoke the admiration of the crowd. Then when the game had been in progress 38 minutes came Barnsley's goal. The movement which produced it began by a

DRAWN BY ERNEST PRATER

TUFNELL SECURING BARNSLEY'S ONE GOAL IN THE GREAT CUP TIE CONTEST AT THE CRYSTAL PALACE

Saturday's fight at the Crystal Palace for the English Football Cup resulted in a draw. Newcastle United and Barnsley each scored a goal, and they were to play again at Goodison Park, the home of the Everton club, on Thursday. It is eight years since the teams in the final round of this extraordinary competition failed to arrive at a definite result; then Sheffield United beat Southampton in the replay. Lord Rosebery, together with hundreds of distinguished spectators, looked on. Away in the distance trees were black with people, young men appeared to be clinging to the frail twigs, inviting serious mishap. Both before and after the match the streets of London were invaded by companies and battalions of green-capped youths wearing either the black of Newcastle or the red of Barnsley.

This montage of images was published to commemorate the Newcastle v Barnsley Cup Final at Crystal Palace and features Tufnall's goal. Wood Collection

good return by Downs, which let in Glendenning, who passed on to Gadsby. The last named, running through, passed to Bartrop, who dodging Whitsun swung the ball over to the left, where Lillycrop unable to shoot himself, touched the ball to Tufnell who managed, in a manner which took Lawrence by surprise, to turn the ball in, with the result that a rather simple shot beat the Newcastle custodian and just inside the post. It was a well-worked goal and brought delight to the hearts of the Barnsley excursionists, but it seemed rather rough on Newcastle after having had the best of the play, thus, to find themselves behind. Moreover, it seemed to me that Lawrence might have been equal to the task of saving Tufnell's shot. After this reverse Newcastle put more dash into their play, and from a beautiful centre by Wilson Shepherd headed in but Mearns who appeared far more confident in his manner of 'keeping' than his vis-à-vis coolly cleared.

The Yorkshire citadel however had a narrow escape when Rutherford swept in and attempted to head through, and with Mearns helpless the ball went only a few inches too high. Thus when half time arrived, Barnsley were leading by a goal, and enjoyed a goodly chance of victory.

Altered Tactics
Changing ends, Newcastle altered the arrangement of their forward line, Wilson and Higgins, their left wing pair, changing places with each other. They henceforward played a more open game. Play grew vigorous and was fairly even and there were several stoppages owing to players on both sides taking hard knocks, Boyle and Bartrop on the Barnsley side especially suffering. Newcastle strove desperately but unmethodically against a great defence, for Downs and Ness continued to show fine form and at length a shot from McWilliam was touched by Shepherd and it flashed intro the net with the referee's whistle sounding for offside against the Newcastle centre. Occasionally the Yorkshiremen came away with a sweeping rush, but their main object now was to defend and hold on to the lead they had got. Against the spirited rushes of the Newcastle forwards the Barnsley halves did sound work and Boyle usually got the better of the bustling Shepherd. The question which everybody was now asking was-would Barnsley hold on to the lead they enjoy?

The Equalser
For a long time it seemed the Yorkshireman would succeed in their efforts, but it was not to be. About ten minutes from time came Newcastle's equaliser, and it cannot be said they did not deserve it. Taking a fine long pass by Veitch, Higgins on the extreme left wing, swung the ball across and Rutherford, dashing into the centre, skilfully seized a golden opportunity of heading past Mearns.

Some people in a line with the play think Rutherford was offside but the location of the Press-box is so unfavourable for seeing the play at the end of the ground where the incident took place that I cannot offer an opinion. The delight of the Newcastle players at the equalisation knew no bounds, and Rutherford was smothered in congratulations similar to those which had almost overwhelmed Tufnell when he did the trick for Barnsley in the first half. So fiercely did the Tynesiders play after this that it seemed possible they might snatch a winning goal in the few minutes that remained and excitement thrilled the serried nasals of the great throng of onlookers. But that grand defence of the Yorkshireman was not to be broken, and although the Novocastrians got several corners, one, indeed, with the very last kick of the game, the red and white heroes of Oakwell lived to fight another day.

Newcastle: Jimmy Lawrence, Billy McCracken, Tony Whiston, Colin Veitch [captain] Wilf Low, Peter McWilliam, Jock Rutherford, Jimmy Howe, Sandy Higgins, Albert Shepherd, George Wilson

Barnsley: Fred Mearns, Dickie Downs, Harry Ness, Bob Glendenning, Tommy Boyle [captain], George Utley, Harry Tufnell, George Lillycrop, Ernie Gadsby, Tom Forman, Wilf Bartrop

Referee – JT Ibbotson

Amazingly, both sides were called upon to play a match, or rather matches, in Newcastle's case, in the five days between the match in London and the replay in Liverpool. On the Monday Newcastle beat Bristol City 4-0 at Ashton Gate, whilst on the Tuesday a Barnsley side devoid of any of their cup final players went down 7-0 away at Grimsby Town whilst 24 hours before the replayed final Newcastle lost 4-0 at the home of the new League Champions, Aston Villa.

Programme to commemorate the 1910 FA Cup Final replay. The sixteen-page issue is one of the rarest of FA Cup Final programmes and the last one to appear at auction in 2000 fetched in excess of £6,500. Wood Collection

16 FA Cup Final Replay v Newcastle United

Thursday 28 April 1910: Goodison Park, Liverpool

Newcastle United   2   (Shepherd 52, 62 – penalty)
Barnsley   0
Attendance: 69,090 Referee: JT Ibbotson

Match report from the *Barnsley Independent*:

Thrilling Encounter at Goodison Park

HOW BARNSLEY FELL

By 'Centre-Forward'

Barnsley football team met their masters yesterday. Their eager bands of followers who set off in the morning for Liverpool beaming with hope and brimful of confidence, returned dismally disappointed. The Yorkshiremen fought gallantly but not so skilfully as at the Crystal Palace on Saturday, and were well beaten by opponents who played in a style greatly superior to that which they had displayed in the drawn game. By two goals to none were Barnsley beaten, and this defeat by no means exaggerated the superiority of their foes. Newcastle United conquered them at their own game. The men from the North began yesterday in the whirlwind style wherein they finished the undecided contest in London and although the opposing defence stoutly resisted them for 50 of the 90 minutes they ultimately overpowered it, and ran out worthy winners of a splendid struggle, marked by great pace and power, and prolific of exciting episodes.

A word for the vanquished

The Barnsley men have no need to feel at all ashamed of their defeat. They have done splendidly. Who would have thought when they went to Blackpool in the first round they would make two more journeys into Lancashire, for replays in the semi-final and final? They have not, it is true, won the English Cup at the first time of reaching the ultimate round. Few clubs have, indeed, accomplished such a feat. But they have gained great glory, built up for themselves a fine reputation as Cup fighters of the highest order, and been the means of placing the club in so happy a financial position that the expedients which the directors in the past have had to resort to keep the club going, notably that of selling their best players, no longer need to be adopted. In comparison with their position at the beginning of the season, Barnsley are now a wealthy club.

Praise for the Victors

Turning to consider the doings of Newcastle, every praise must be given to them for the dashing yet skilful football they played yesterday. That they deserved their victory there is not a shadow of a doubt whatsoever. They played the true cup winning game, and played it in a potential and clever manner, and the merit of their performance is greatly enhanced by the adverse conditions under which it was accomplished, for many hours' rain had rendered the ground in a state greatly adverse to good football. Yet the Novocastrians controlled the ball admirably, passed well, shot at goal for the most part accurately and set up not only a sound but also a skilful defence. Indeed they gave a really great display of football under the circumstances - and small was the wonder that Barnsley, plucky a team as they are, found themselves quite outplayed.

A Goalless Half

Although there were some near things at each end and many exciting moments in front of the Barnsley goal, there was no score during the first half, though it was in this period of the game that Newcastle had the wind behind them and occasional flashes of sunshine in the faces of their foes. The great feature of the Newcastle attack was the strength of their left wing, Higgins and Wilson playing splendidly, while Shepherd in the centre manifested a great improvement upon the form he showed at the Palace on Saturday. Although the Yorkshire forwards occasionally flashed away in threatening style, the red and whites were kept mainly on the defensive.

Shepherd's Success

Six minutes after change of ends came the first goal and a very good one it was. Shepherd, the Newcastle opportunist centre, was the hero thereof. It was obtained in his characteristic style. Seeing the ball going ahead, and opening between the two Barnsley backs, he went past them, like a flash, gathered the ball skilfully, and pausing not an instant drive it in fiercely into the net. Barnsley made a bold dash for an equaliser, but never looked like getting it, and the Tynesiders continued strong and persistent in their attacks, a lot being now seen of Rutherford, who had not had much of a show in the first half. The Newcastle men realised that they wanted a second goal in order to make victory secure. They obtained it twenty minutes from the finish, Glendenning tripping McWilliam in the 18 yards area and Shepherd accurately taking the

A Barnsley medal from the 1910 Cup Final. Wood Collecti

penalty kick. It was a great day for Shepherd, who it was thought would perhaps have to stand down for Stewart, and the judgement of the Newcastle directors in again choosing him, especially with the ground in so wet a state, was amply justified. Not only did he shoot two goals. But he came very near doing the hat trick, for near the end he made another of his sudden rushes and shot only a foot wide.

Barnsley Played Down

After Newcastle's second goal it was clear to all that Barnsley were a well-beaten team. In skill, pace, and vigour they were alike outplayed. Mearns did several very smart things in goal, and Downs and Ness, without being as sound as they were in London on Saturday, worked splendidly in defence. Boyle also played excellently at centre-half despite the fact that he failed to hold Shepherd as well as on the former occasion. The Barnsley forwards met their masters in the Newcastle halves, Veitch, Low and McWilliam making a splendid trio. M'Cracken gave another fine display at right back, and Carr was an improvement upon Whitson, Lawrence had not much to do in goal, but he did one very smart thing in turning aside a dangerous shot when he was yards away from his citadel. The Newcastle forwards were splendid. Wilson and Higgins being a great wing in the first half. Indeed Wilson was prominent throughout the game, while Rutherford was conspicuous in the second half.

The Cup Well Won

The success of the Newcastle team was naturally received with great enthusiasm, for they had many supporters present. Moreover, the fine football whereby they had won a splendidly fought game commanded the admiration of all. Success had been a long time in coming to them, for they have had to play in four final ties and replay before gaining their ambition. But now that they have at last won the Cup everyone must agree that they thoroughly deserve it. There was a great display of enthusiasm

A rare souvenir Colman's Mustard vesta produced to commemorate Newcastle United's 1910 FA Cup victory. Colman's Mustard

This 'funeral' card was a mean way to illustrate Barnsley's defeat in 1910. Wood Collection

at the close when they received the coveted trophy at the hands of the Earl of Derby. There was a magnificent attendance despite the wet weather, which continued right up to the beginning of the game, fully 60,000 people being present and the receipts amounting to £4,166.

Newcastle: Jimmy Lawrence, Billy McCracken, Jack Carr, Colin Veitch (captain) Wilf Low, Peter McWilliam, Jock Rutherford, Jimmy Howe, Sandy Higgins, Albert Shepherd, George Wilson

Barnsley: Fred Mearns, Dickie Downs, Harry Ness, Bob Glendenning, Tommy Boyle [captain], George Utley, Harry Tufnell, George Lillycrop, Ernie Gadsby, Tom Forman, Wilf Bartrop

1909/1910

9th in Division Two
P38 W16 D7 L15 F62 A59

	Date	Opponents	Res	Att	Goalscorers	Cooper JC	Downs JT	Ness HM	Glendenning R	Boyle TW	Utley G	Coulthard ET	Gadsby E	Lillycrop GB	Hellewell Alec	Forman T	Bartrop W	Tufnell H	Taylor JH	Biggins FJ	Oxspring A	Mearns FC	Little J	Martin F	Arthurs G	Graham TH	Kay H	Jebb A	Ellis EE	Wren C
1	**2-Sep H**	**Hull City**	**1 - 2**	**5,000**	**Lillycrop**	1	2	3	4	5	6	7	8	9	10	11														
2	4-Sep A	Glossop	0 - 3			1	2	3	4	5	6		8	9		11	7	10												
3	**11-Sep H**	**Birmingham**	**5 - 1**	**3,000**	**Lillycrop 2, Tufnell, Gadsby, Forman**	1	2	3	4	5	6		8	9		11	7	10												
4	18-Sep A	West Bromwich Albion	3 - 4	10,000	Lillycrop 2, Boyle	1	2	3	4	5	6		8	9		11	7	10												
5	**25-Sep H**	**Oldham Athletic**	**2 - 1**	**4,000**	**Gadsby, Taylor**	1	2	3	4	5	6		8	9		11	7		10											
6	**2-Oct H**	**Bradford Park Avenue**	**4 - 0**	**6,000**	**Tufnell 2, Forman, Lillycrop**	1	2	3	4	5	6		8	9		11	7	10												
7	9-Oct A	Fulham	0 - 3	20,000		1	2	3	4	5	6		8	9		11	7	10												
8	11-Oct A	Hull City	0 - 1	8,000		1	2	3	4	5	6		8	9		11	7	10												
9	**16-Oct H**	**Burnley**	**0 - 0**	**4,000**		1	2	3	4	5	6		9			11		10	8	7										
10	23-Oct A	Leeds City	7 - 0	8,000	Gadsby 2, Lillycrop 2, Tufnell 2, Forman	1	2	3	4	5	6		8	9		11		10		7										
11	**30-Oct H**	**Wolverhampton Wanderers**	**7 - 1**	**5,500**	**Gadsby 3, Boyle, Lillycrop, Forman, Bartrop**	1	2	3	4	5	6		8	9		11	7	10												
12	6-Nov A	Gainsborough Trinity	0 - 0			1	2	3	4	5	6		8	9		11	7	10												
13	**13-Nov H**	**Grimsby Town**	**2 - 1**	**5,000**	**Lillycrop, Tufnell**	1	2	3	4	5	6		8	9		11	7	10												
14	**27-Nov H**	**Leicester Fosse**	**3 - 1**	**6,000**	**Gadsby, Tufnell, Lillycrop**	1	2	3	4	5	6		8	9		11	7	10												
15	**11-Dec H**	**Clapton Orient**	**2 - 1**		**Gadsby, Lillycrop**	1	2	3	4				8	9	5	11	7	10			6									
16	18-Dec A	Blackpool	0 - 0			1	2	3	4	5	6		8	9		11	7	10												
17	25-Dec A	Derby County	1 - 2	15,000	Lillycrop	1	2	3	4	5	6		8	9		11	7	10												
18	**27-Dec H**	**Stockport County**	**1 - 0**		**Lillycrop**	1	2	3	4	5	6		8	9		11	7	10												
19	**28-Dec H**	**Derby County**	**5 - 1**	**10,126**	**Lillycrop 2, Boyle 2, Gadsby**	1	2	3	4	5	6		8	9		11	7	10												
20	1-Jan A	Stockport County	0 - 5	5,000			2	3	4		5		8	9		11	7	10	6			1								
21	**8-Jan H**	**Glossop**	**3 - 0**	**8,000**	**Lillycrop 2, Boyle**		2	3	4	5	6		8	9		11	7	10				1								
22	22-Jan A	Birmingham	1 - 2	5,000	Boyle		2	3	4	5	6		8	9		11	7	10				1								
23	12-Feb A	Bradford Park Avenue	0 - 2	12,000		1	2	3	4		6		8	9	5	11	7	10												
24	**24-Feb H**	**Fulham**	**2 - 1**	**3,000**	**Lillycrop, Forman**		2	3	4	5	6		8	9		11	7	10				1								
25	26-Feb A	Burnley	0 - 2	3,000				3	4	5	6		8				7	10				1	2	9	11					
26	9-Mar A	Manchester City	0 - 0	15,000			2	3	4	5	6		8	9		11	7	10				1								
27	12-Mar A	Wolverhampton Wanderers	0 - 1	5,000			2	3	4	5	6		8			11	7					1				9	10			
28	14-Mar A	Oldham Athletic	0 - 5	6,000		1		3		5	6	10	8		9		7		4				2		11					
29	**17-Mar H**	**Leeds City**	**1 - 1**	**3,000**	**Gadsby**	1	2	3	4	5	6		8	9		11	7	10												
30	**19-Mar H**	**Gainsborough Trinity**	**4 - 1**	**3,000**	**Boyle (Pen), Coulthard, Kay, Lillycrop**	1	2	3		5	6			9			7	11	8								10	4		
31	**28-Mar H**	**Lincoln City**	**2 - 1**		**Taylor, Hellewell**	1						11			9				8	5	6		2	7			10		3	[illegible]
32	**2-Apr H**	**Manchester City**	**1 - 1**	**10,000**	**Gadsby**		2	3	4	5	6		8	9		11	7	10				1								
33	7-Apr A	Clapton Orient	0 - 4	4,000			2		4		6	10		9		11	7		8			1						5	3	
34	9-Apr A	Leicester Fosse	1 - 1		Lillycrop			3		5	6			9		11	7	10	8	4		1	2							
35	**14-Apr H**	**West Bromwich Albion**	**2 - 1**	**2,500**	**Forman, Bartrop**			3	4	5	6		8	9		11	7	10				1							2	
36	16-Apr A	Lincoln City	1 - 2	6,000	Lillycrop			3	4	5	6		8	9		11	7	10				1							2	
37	26-Apr A	Grimsby Town	0 - 7	2,000		1									9				8	4	11		3	7			10	5	2	[illegible]
38	**30-Apr H**	**Blackpool**	**1 - 0**	**3,000**	**Lillycrop**		2	3	4	5	6		8	9		11	7	10				1								
FA Cup																														
R1	15-Jan A	Blackpool	1 - 1	8,000	Tufnell		2	3	4	5	6		8	9		11	7	10				1								
R1r	**20-Jan H**	**Blackpool**	**6 - 0**	**13,939**	**Lillycrop 2, Tufnell 2, Gadsby, Boyle (Pen)**		2	3	4	5	6		8	9		11	7	10				1								
R2	**5-Feb H**	**Bristol Rovers**	**4 - 0**	**10,285**	**Bartrop, Gadsby, Forman, Utley**	1	2	3	4	5	6		8	9		11	7	10												
R3	**19-Feb H**	**West Bromwich Albion**	**1 - 0**	**18,636**	**Tufnell**	1	2	3	4	5	6		8	9		11	7	10												
R4	**5-Mar H**	**Queens Park Rangers**	**1 - 0**	**23,574**	**Bartrop 24**		2	3	4	5	6		8	9		11	7	10				1								
SF	26-Mar N	Everton	0 - 0	35,000	(Elland Road)		2	3	4	5	6		8	9		11	7	10				1								
SFr	31-Mar N	Everton	3 - 0	55,000	Gadsby, Forman, Tufnell (Old Trafford)		2	3	4	5	6		8	9		11	7	10				1								
Fin	23-Apr N	Newcastle United	1 - 1	77,747	Tufnell (Crystal Palace)		2	3	4	5	6		8	9		11	7	10				1								
Finr	28-Apr N	Newcastle United	0 - 2	69,090	(Goodison Park) £4166		2	3	4	5	6		8	9		11	7	10				1								
			League Apps			25	31	35	33	32	35	4	33	32	6	33	33	31	9	5	3	13	5	3	2	1	4	3	5	[illegible]
			Goals							7		1	12	23	1	6	2	7	2								1			
			FA Cup Apps			2	9	9	9	9	9	0	9	9	0	9	9	9	0	0	0	7	0	0	0	0	0	0	0	[illegible]
			Goals							1	1		3	2		2	2	6												

17 The 1910 European Tour

After the near success of the 1910 final the club's name came to the attention of the footballing world and following the trend set by a number of professional clubs, negotiations were made for a tour of the Continent. A party consisting of thirteen players plus manager Arthur Fairclough, trainer Bill Norman and director Percy Waite departed on Wednesday 5 May 1910 for a tour that would see eleven games in five countries over twenty-seven days. The group left Barnsley station at 8.30am and by means of train, charabanc, train, steamer, train and taxis arrived at the Grand Hotel Du Louve Paris at 9.30pm. The journey had been long but fairly uneventful with Lillycrop being the only player to suffer a bout of 'mal de mere' on the one-and-a-half-hour sea crossing. It was approaching midnight when they were finished with their evening meal so retired on the day exhausted.

The next afternoon saw a challenge match with Swindon Town at the Parc des Princes ground for the Dubonnet Cup. The fixture had been arranged by the French Football Union to promote the game in the country and a huge three-foot bronze trophy was to be offered to the winners. Originally they had hoped to have the two Cup finalists to play the game, but Newcastle were unavailable so the Wiltshire club, who had been defeated by the Magpies in the semi final, were invited to take their place. The ground was some four miles from the hotel so this involved a motor-bus journey passing down some of the most beautiful avenues that are unique to Paris and a fine reception awaited the squad. Barnsley selected the team that had lost the final with the exception of goalkeeper George Wilcock who replaced Mearns and they played a wonderful game and fully deserved to win, but they could not beat Skiller in the Swindon goal who was in fine form.

The team rained down shots onto the Robins goal but the keeper seemed to charm the ball by stopping attempts from all angles. Billy Silto, the former Reds centre half, played a very determined game and in Harold Fleming, the English International forward, the opposition had a natural goalscorer who took his two chances with ease. Lillycrop scored the first goal of the tour and as the Reds pressed the game for an equaliser, Dickie Downs missed a penalty. At the game's conclusion captain Boyle could not hide his disappointment with the 2-1 score line and this was mirrored by the squad as Swindon were presented with gold medals of the occasion. The defeat could be partly attributed to the long and tiring journey of the day before and of course the Reds would gain their revenge in the 1912 semi-final. Throughout the game, the Dubonnet Cup had been guarded by a single gendarme with a drawn sword and at its presentation it took two people to carry it off. Overall the organisers were delighted with the spectacle as nothing like it had been seen in Paris before and despite the rainy conditions a crowd of 7,000 had paid some 6,000 francs at the gate. After the game the teams were entertained at the Alhambra by the Paris Football Union and later Mr Robert Desmarets the editor of *L'Auto* took the whole party to the Theatre Follies Berger. Although they did not understand a word of the opera, the singing, staging and dresses were something never to be forgotten and all the boys were delighted at the elaborate show. The following morning Mr Desmarets organised a trip on a steamer down the River Seine and seven miles of beautiful sailing and scenery was enjoyed for a cost of two pence each. After nearly an hour's run, the party disembarked at St Cloud and walked through the lovely palace of Napoleon Bonaparte. The grounds and lakes were most magnificent and the park keeper was persuaded to start the great waterfall and fountains for the players' special benefit. A visit to the National Monumental Works followed where workmen displayed various ceramic skills but the opportunity to buy one of the tea sets for £100 was not taken up. From here the company took a six-mile tram ride to the Palace at Versailles and after two hours of walking around they adjourned

to a hostelry where Harry Tufnell tried his hand at the language. He ordered a snack of bread and cheese from a waitress and there was much merriment in the party when she returned with a jam tart.

The next morning they left Paris for a 400-mile train journey to Karlsruhe which took fully nine hours to complete but it was never considered monotonous due to the beautiful scenery. German club officials met the train and after a hearty meal in the hotel

Captain Tommy Boyle and his Swindon counterpart Charlie Bannister pose with the match referee prior to the Dubonnet Cup match, Parc de Princes, Paris, 5 May 1910. Wood Collection

Dubonnet Cup winner's medal.
The Dubonnet Cup. Wood Collection

they showed the party around the town where the feeling was that this was 'an easy going place'. The next day was a match day and it was announced that the King, Edward VII, had died. This saddened the players greatly and it was quickly arranged to play the game wearing black armbands. It was also a Sunday and the body of men were amazed at the novelty of the shops and cafes remaining open on the Sabbath. They were fascinated to see vending machines where for a penny German beers, soft drinks, cherry brandy, light wines, cakes, buns, sandwiches and even sardines on toast could be dispensed and it was felt that England was sadly behind the times. The match was played some four miles from the centre of the city and Barnsley were warned by the old English international Billy Townley that it would be a tough encounter. He was coaching in the city and stated that the opponents Karlsruhe Phoenix Club were probably the best club in Germany but they need not have worried. Although the Germans played well they were no match for the Reds who ran out easy winners six goals to nil. Early in the game, Gadsby sustained a nasty one-inch cut on his head that had to be stitched up and when he returned to the fray he grabbed three goals. Tufnell with two and Bartrop completed the scoring and at the conclusion of the game the victors were simply worshipped by the crowd, opposing players and officials alike. They were invited down to the club rooms and were told they could have anything they wanted for the whole of the evening at their hosts' expense. The players were looked upon as marvels with Tom Forman, who had played a great game, the centre of attention. They looked upon him as something unnatural by the way he ran down the wing and centred accurately every time and just like the Parisians before them, had never seen such football before. All six goals came from his centres with the exception of the first, which was a Bartrop masterpiece. A very strange feature of the game was that the netting for the goals was made from woven wire instead of the regular twine. It was of the same mesh but stretched very tight and Barnsley officials informed their counterparts that this was very dangerous especially for the goalkeepers. A sad postscript to the visit was that Karlsruhe would later become Barnsley opponents on a much larger scale with tragic results. In 1916 the two battalions of Barnsley Pals would be dug in on the Somme in direct opposition with 169th Light Infantry that was based in the German city. The proceeding two years would see both sides succeed in despatching much of its opposition's menfolk into oblivion around the French town of Serre.

An early start again awaited the party the next morning for the 800-mile, two-day journey to Graz. Stopping off at Munich to change trains and Salzburg for the evening, they arrived at their destination after midnight and were quick to retire to bed. In the morning some of their opponents came to the hotel and conducted the team on a tour of the city. A rocky outcrop dominated the skyline and after climbing to the top the group were presented with panoramic view that took their breath away. As well as presenting a bird's eye view of the beautiful rooftops of Graz and the river Mur flowing below, in the distance could be seen the imposing Alps. There were fine gardens and cafes on the top of this small mountain and after taking in the sights the party took advantage of the cliff railway, which was similar to the one at Scarborough but longer, to descend the mountain. In the afternoon Barnsley were driven to the ground in carriages where they were warmly welcomed by their opponents AC Graz. As far as the game is concerned it would be fair to say that it was a complete mis-match as the visitors ran out winners by 12 goals to two. The scorers were Tufnell, six, Utley, four, with Lillycrop and Forman getting one each and although both the opposition's goals were gifted, it soothed them greatly and it put them in a good temperament. It was also noted that nearly every one of opposition's players carried deep duelling scars on their faces and that in these parts no one was considered brave without them. After the game they returned to the top of the mountain and were royally entertained by their hosts. Everything was provided free for the benefit of the visitors and a jolly night was had by all. The next morning's paper carried a lengthy report of the game and was full of favourable comments. The event drew a record crowd and would have a special place in the history of Graz sport. The locals were also delighted with their performance against what was obviously 'One of the finest teams in the World'.

The following afternoon saw a beautiful train journey to Vienna where the twisting and turning track gave the impression you could easily shake hands with the driver. After an overnight stop the party moved on to Budapest where they had arranged the gruelling task of three matches in three days. They were met at the station by several important Hungarian football officials, who gave the impression of being very wealthy people. The president of one of the clubs was entertaining the great wrestler George Hackensmidt and he was to be in the company of the players for the weekend's games. The weather was quite tropical and at one stage the players thought they may die from the heat but a feature of the area was the thunderstorms which broke quickly and in torrents. In the day they were shown the world's first underground electric underground railway and the courts of justice by their footballing friends and they then ventured over the Danube suspension bridge to see the changing of the guard in the Palace grounds. It was a very hot morning, and they were nearly boiled when they reached their destination which was situated hundreds of feet below the river level. On the return journey it commenced to rain and kept it up just before kick-off of the first game in the afternoon. Barnsley's first opponents were Hungary's oldest club Budapest Gymnastic Club or B.T.C. as they were known and they were easily brushed aside five goals to one. Tufnell and Lillycrop both scored a brace and Boyle hit a penalty as the Reds played their strongest team. When they came to the ground it was covered in pools of standing water some three inches in depth and it was so deep in fact that the players washed their hands in it. The unfortunate Ernest Gadsby was soon in the thick of it again when a few of opposition's players, who were in the main very physical, upturned him into one of these pools. He emerged from it looking like a drowned rat but worse was to follow, later he had half his shirt torn from his back and finished the game with another nasty cut over his eye which required him to leave the field and require assistance from a doctor.

On Sunday they were taken for a drive around the town where they viewed the various places of interest, finishing with a lovely ride through the main park. The weather was ideal but in the afternoon the storm broke with the most unmerciful rain right up to the advertised kick-off of 5pm. When they arrived at the ground they could not quite believe their eyes, the centre of the field was quite easily six inches deep in water. The officials of the Hungarian Gymnastic Club or M.T.K. came into the dressing rooms and begged the team not to turn out for 20 or 30 minutes until they had got the water off. Peter Waite could not see how this was to be done and followed the hosts to watch the process. The pitch had no turf on it and consisted entirely of sand and digging down a few inches revealed a huge wooden lid to a drain which, when removed, allowed gallons of water to flow away. A crowd of around 8,000 had gathered despite the weather and Barnsley had been warned these opponents would 'take them all the way' but that was far from the mark. The visitors won by seven goals to nil and played their hosts to a standstill with Tom Forman and Frank Biggins scoring two goals each. Bartrop, Tufnell and Lillycrop completed the rout and the homesters could only look on as the Reds marched towards goal. After the match the team received a fantastic reception from the crowd with cries of 'Bravo, England' ringing out.

Monday's hosts were the five times champions of Hungary Ferencvaros, or F.T.C. and the weather turned out to be a day of almost unbearable heat. The two previous games (no matter how easy they were) had taken their toll and coupled with the conditions and their opponents, Barnsley lost to foreign opposition for the only time on the tour. A crowd of around 12,000 warmly welcomed the visitors on to the field and from the off it looked as though they would continue their high scoring ways. In the first minutes the Hungarian goal was hard pressed, but the keeper saved miraculously. Then a moment later, a speedy attack by the host's left wing saw his exact centre converted for the first goal. A tremendous cheering and hand clapping greeted the goal but this was soon silenced as the Yorkshiremen pressed for the equaliser. First Tom Forman's incisive running forced a series of corners and on 14 minutes from the other wing Wilf Bartrop's whipped-in centre glanced off the boot of a defender for the equaliser. Barnsley were in the ascendancy now but a pacy breakaway again down the left, saw the winger exchange passes and put across a perfect centre for the forward to score. The defenders protested and appealed for offside but it had been a lightning counter attack that had taken them by surprise. The game was played in a much fairer spirit that the previous two matches but it was severely tested more than once. The home trainer had thoughtfully placed a pail of cool lemon water by the touchline to quench the thirsts of his team in the heat. Throughout the match players were constantly leaving the field for refreshment while Barnsley soldiered on manfully. Eventually the injustice became too much for captain Tommy Boyle who with a huge kick sent juice flying in all directions. Naturally this caused concern among the partisan home crowd and more was to follow. From a free-kick the Ferencvaros keeper threw himself upon the ball and Lillycrop rushed in to try to kick it in the goal. The forward must have caught him on the head and the referee gave him a stern warning despite George vigorously protesting

The Hungarian team, possibly Ferencvaros or 'Francetown' (as Barnsley officials called them) that played Barnsley on their European tour. Wood Collection

The Barnsley team in Budapest. Bower Collection

his innocence. The crowd also were again none too pleased and tried to sway the official but after a few minutes the keeper recovered enough for the game to be resumed. In the second half the pace slackened a little as the visitors began to tire but none the less they put all their remaining strength into levelling the game. Unfortunately they were up against a green and white defence that had given an almost faultless performance and behind them was an inspired goalkeeper who had pulled of many beautiful saves. At the end of the game the victorious home team was cheered frantically from the field and it was agreed that in the history of Hungarian football they had never seen such a game of football or a Hungarian performance to match this day. The Barnsley officials felt that the hosts possessed many men who would not be out of place in the English league and that this game had done football in Hungary a great deal of good and would be remembered for many years to come.

On Tuesday afternoon the Barnsley assembly moved back to Vienna for a spell of two games in six days with the weather still unbearably hot. Wednesday's opponents were a select side drawn from the three best teams in the city playing under the name 'the Vienna Cricket and Athletic Club' and after the Hungarian exertions everyone anticipated a tough encounter. Thankfully, the kick off at 6pm avoided the height of the sun but the players were still in quite a state with the conditions and tired from having spent their rest day travelling in the heat. Within minutes of the start of the game it soon became apparent that the players would not have a hard task defeating the Austrians and simply toyed with them, tapping the ball from one to another in easy going style. A feature of the refereeing in this part of world was not to allow any contact with the player in possession of the ball. This resulted in the whistle constantly being blown and the crowd baying for fouls that never existed. This led to an unpleasant incident in the second half where through some misunderstanding the referee walked off the field and so stopped the game. After 15 minutes a replacement was found and tried to restart the game immediately but some of the Barnsley players had started to get changed so there was a further delay. Eventually the game did resume, with the visitors leading 3-1 through Bartrop, Gadsby and Boyle but it was now quite dark and almost impossible to follow the ball. A further goal for the Reds was inexplicably disallowed and rather than leave the field in protest they decided to dally the time away on the field until time was called. Following the game the party had their longest break in the tour from football of three full days. The World's First Hunting Exhibition (Die Internationale Jagd-Ausstellung) was being held in the city and this occupied a fair amount of their time and the entire group were happy not to be playing a match on Friday as this was the King's funeral. Vienna Sports Club was the last of their Austrian opponents and a fairly uneventful game saw the Reds run out 5-3 winners.

After the delights of the Austro-Hungarian Empire the troop began their long journey home by stopping off in Prague. The city in this time was regarded as the finest in Europe and contained some truly wonderful sites namely the Cathedral of St Vitus and the Silver shrine of St John Nepomucene. Also they were shown round the ancient Jewish synagogue and cemetery which dated back to 592 AD and their guide instructed them that up until 20 years ago a chain was drawn around the area to keep the Jews from coming into the centre of the city in the evening. As well as the native Bohemians, the city contained a large population of Germans and it was the Deutsch Football Club that would be the next opponents. The match itself was the most interesting and gentlemanly of the all those played on the continent and despite being told that this was another German team that was going to take them to the limit, the visitors ran out winners five goals to nil. The team played a very clean and tricky game and fairly dazzled the spectators and Tom Forman was distinct in his running and shooting. The combination play was perfect and it was felt that had the goalkeeper not been an un-natural being the score would have been nearer twenty.

A delightful six-hour train journey took the contingent to Leipzig and some members commented that they must be getting nearer to home as this was the coldest they'd been for a fortnight. The ground of their opponents the Leipzig Sports Club was splendidly situated in the country about 25 minutes' drive from the hotel and possessed a very nice playing pitch. Prior to the kick off they spent a pleasant 20 minutes watching the world champion cyclist practising on a great cement track. He was being paced by a motor cycle, and at one time was travelling at a rate of over 60 miles per hour. The hosts were a fine body of chaps and kept the visitors at bay for quite some time. Once again Barnsley came up against a fine keeper and eventually ran out 5-1 winners with Lillycrop and Gadsby grabbing a brace each and Tufnell completing the score. The game was an evening kick-off and at its conclusion they had very little time to feed and then catch the 10pm train to their next destination.

'Dickie' Downs portrayed on a Baines' trade card.
Wood Collection

The final game of the tour had been arranged for the next day in Hamburg and this obliged the party to make the seven-and-a-half-hour journey by night. They arrived at 5.30am none the worse for the experience having managed a sleep in the comfortable carriages and after rolls and coffee retired to bed until early afternoon. The game was a very tame affair with the visitors hardly getting into a trot for their 2-0 victory. Forman and Gadsby were the scorers and although the team was clearly showing the tiredness of the tour, the home spectators were pleased with the spectacle.

The next afternoon the group embarked on the eight-hour trip to the Hook of Holland for the night boat to Harwich. The weather on the crossing was extremely rough and the voyage was anything but pleasant and once back in the old country they were ready for a hearty breakfast. Good time was made on the journey back to Barnsley where they were met by a number of friends and admirers at the Court House Station some 25 hours after leaving Hamburg.

In conclusion, the Barnsley tourists had undertaken an unforgettable month of experiences and had returned with a record of nine wins from the eleven games. They had scored fifty-two goals and conceded just twelve and had been received with great courtesy everywhere they had played. Overall the tour had made a loss of £158 1s 10d but everything had passed off without great incident and the players would have many pleasant memories of their enjoyable tour.

PART FOUR

SEASON 1910-11

After such a brilliant season, from both a playing and financial aspect, there was general approval amongst the supporters when it was announced that all the cup squad had been re-signed for the forthcoming campaign. All the signs were there that this was to be another successful season with a possible push for promotion, so in retrospect when judging returns against expectations, this must easily rank as the most disappointing in the club's history.

Despite a squad of talents, injuries and the loss of form meant the club were never able to field the 1910 Cup Final side. A return of just five points from the opening ten games saw Barnsley in 19th place and struggling. The young forward Ernest Gadsby was the first casualty of this alarming decline and saw himself initially dropped to the reserves. By the end of November, Fred Mearns who had little competition for his place owing to a season-long injury to keeper Jack Cooper, was also dropped. He was replaced by the Bristol City keeper John Clegg who had been exchanged for the faltering Gadsby. January saw the obviously unhappy Mearns moving on to Leicester Fosse with the much-travelled forward George Travers making the opposite journey. He was to make only intermittent appearances for the team as they failed to find the consistency needed to produce results. The following month saw the departure of Tom Forman from the club to join First Division Tottenham Hotspur who were fighting a relegation battle. Tom had been an ever present on the left wing up to his transfer and the introduction of his understudy George Arthurs finally saw an upturn in form. Arthurs had previously played with Bartrop at Worksop Town and although on opposite wings, their play seemed to complement each other and the team's fortunes.

From a mid March position of being marooned at the bottom of the league, the team went on a run of one defeat in the final ten games to avoid the wooden spoon. The strong finish was not enough to avoid having to apply for re-election although it was a close thing. With one game to go Barnsley were two places above the zone but a 5-1 defeat at Derby coupled with wins for two of their closest rivals saw the hard work of the previous six weeks undone. So a mere 12 months on from being minutes away from an FA Cup final victory, the club would have to go cap in hand to the League for the second time in its history.

From a financial point of view, the club lost £1,255 (£71,600 today) over the previous twelve months but when you consider the increase in expenditure, this was a satisfactory outcome. Over £1,000 extra had been offered in wages to the Cup Final players, £130 had been paid in bonuses and the European tour had lost £158. One pleasing aspect was that gate receipts did not suffer despite the lack of success on the field. Both first team and reserve fixtures showed a marked increase and provided returns of over £3,500.

When the result of the vote from the Football League AGM was announced a few weeks after the end of the season, Barnsley had been re-elected in first place well in front of their nearest challengers. The member clubs had recognised what a disappointing season this had been and it would have been the cruellest of blows if the club had lost their League place at the end of a year that had promised so much.

1910/1911

19th in Division Two
P38 W7 D14 L17 F52 A62
Re-Elected

No	Date	Opponents	Res	Att	Goalscorers	Mearns FC	Downs JT	Ness HM	Glendenning R	Utley G	Jebb A	Bartrop W	Gadsby E	Lillycrop GB	Tufnell H	Forman T	Martin F	Bratley PW	Birtles TJ	Boyle TW	Taylor JH	Ellis EE	Biggins FJ	Rutter A	Clegg JA	Travers JE	Arthurs G	Johnson P	Little J
1	3-Sep H	Wolverhampton Wanderers	2 - 2	5,000	Lillycrop, Forman	1	2	3	4	5	6	7	8	9	10	11													
2	10-Sep A	Chelsea	1 - 3	21,000	Gadsby	1	2	3	4	5	6	7	8		10	11	9												
3	17-Sep H	Clapton Orient	1 - 2	5,500	Martin	1	2	3	4	5	6	7	8		10	11	9												
4	24-Sep A	Blackpool	0 - 1	7,000		1	2	3	4	6			8	9	10	11		5	7										
5	1-Oct H	Glossop	4 - 0		Forman, Lillycrop 2, Birtles	1	2	3	4	6			8	9	10	11		5	7										
6	8-Oct A	Lincoln City	0 - 1			1	2	3	4	6			8	9	10	11			7	5									
7	22-Oct A	Birmingham	0 - 1	10,000		1	2	3		6		7	10	9		11		4		5	8								
8	26-Oct A	Gainsborough Trinity	1 - 1		Taylor	1	2			6		7	10	9		11		4		5	8	3							
9	29-Oct H	West Bromwich Albion	1 - 1	5,000	Taylor	1	2		4	6		7	10	9		11				5	8	3							
10	5-Nov A	Hull City	1 - 5	7,000	Tufnell	1	2	3	4	6		7		9	10	11				5	8								
11	12-Nov H	Fulham	4 - 2	5,000	Lillycrop, Taylor 2 (1 Pen), Tufnell	1	2	3	4	6				9	10	11			7	5	8								
12	17-Nov H	Huddersfield Town	1 - 2	2,000	Tufnell	1	2	3		6				9	10	11			7	5	8		4						
13	19-Nov A	Bradford Park Avenue	3 - 2	12,000	Rutter 2, Tufnell	1	2	3		6				8	10	11		4		5			7	9					
14	26-Nov H	Burnley	0 - 1	4,000		1	2	3		6				8	10	11		4		5			7	9					
15	10-Dec H	Leeds City	4 - 0	4,000	Bartrop, Boyle, Lillycrop, Forman		2	3		6				8	10	11		4		5			7	9	1				
16	17-Dec A	Stockport County	2 - 2	2,500	Rutter, Lillycrop		2	3		6				8	10	11				5			4	9	1				
17	24-Dec H	Derby County	0 - 2	5,000			2	3		6				8	10	11				5			4	9	1				
18	27-Dec A	Leicester Fosse	1 - 1	15,000	Forman (Pen)		2	3	4	6				8	10	11				5				9	1				
19	31-Dec A	Wolverhampton Wanderers	0 - 1	7,000			2	3	4	6		7		8	10	11				5	9				1				
20	2-Jan A	Bolton Wanderers	0 - 4				2	3	4	6		7		9	10	11				5	8				1				
21	7-Jan H	Chelsea	3 - 2	7,000	Boyle, Lillycrop, Tufnell		2	3	4	6		7		9	10	11				5	8				1				
22	21-Jan A	Clapton Orient	0 - 3	8,000			2	3	4	6		7		9	10	11				5					1	8			
23	28-Jan H	Blackpool	1 - 2	5,000	Tufnell		2	3	4		6	7		9	10	11				5					1	8			
24	11-Feb H	Lincoln City	2 - 2		Tufnell, Rutter			3	4	6				8	10	11				5		2	7	9	1				
25	18-Feb A	Huddersfield Town	0 - 2	8,000			2	3	4	6				8	10			5					7	9	1		11		
26	25-Feb H	Birmingham	2 - 3	2,500	Arthurs, Tufnell		2	3	4	6					10					5			7	9	1	8	11		
27	4-Mar A	West Bromwich Albion	3 - 3	8,000	Lillycrop, Rutter, Tufnell		2		4	6		7		10				5						9	1	8	11	3	
28	11-Mar H	Hull City	0 - 1	5,000			2	3	4	6		7		8				5						9	1	10	11		
29	18-Mar A	Fulham	2 - 0	8,000	Biggins, Bartrop		2		4	6					10			7		5			8	9	1		11		3
30	25-Mar H	Bradford Park Avenue	7 - 0	4,000	Lillycrop 3, Tufnell 2, Utley, Bartrop		2		4	6		7		9	10					5			8		1		11		3
31	28-Mar A	Glossop	1 - 1		Arthurs		2		4	6		7		9	10					5			8		1		11		3
32	1-Apr A	Burnley	0 - 0	4,000			2		4	6		7		9	10					5			8		1		11		3
33	8-Apr H	Gainsborough Trinity	2 - 2		Tufnell, Biggins		2		4	6		7		9	10					5			8		1		11		3
34	14-Apr H	Leicester Fosse	1 - 1	6,000	Tufnell		2		4	6		7		9	10					5			8		1		11		3
35	15-Apr A	Leeds City	0 - 0	10,000			2	3	4	6		7		9	10					5				8	1		11		
36	17-Apr H	Bolton Wanderers	0 - 0				2	3	4	6		7		9	10					5				8	1		11		
37	22-Apr H	Stockport County	1 - 1	3,000	Tufnell		2	3	4	6		7		9	10					5				8	1		11		
38	29-Apr A	Derby County	1 - 5	5,000	Taylor		2	3	4			7		9	10			6		5	8				1		11		

FA Cup

No	Date	Opponents	Res	Att	Goalscorers	Mearns FC	Downs JT	Ness HM	Glendenning R	Utley G	Jebb A	Bartrop W	Gadsby E	Lillycrop GB	Tufnell H	Forman T	Martin F	Bratley PW	Birtles TJ	Boyle TW	Taylor JH	Ellis EE	Biggins FJ	Rutter A	Clegg JA	Travers JE	Arthurs G	Johnson P	Little J
R1	14-Jan A	Watford	2 - 0	6,000	Lillycrop, Boyle		2	3	4	6		7		9	10	11				5	8				1				
R2	4-Feb A	Burnley	0 - 2				2	3	4	6		7		9	10	11				5			8		1				

	Mearns FC	Downs JT	Ness HM	Glendenning R	Utley G	Jebb A	Bartrop W	Gadsby E	Lillycrop GB	Tufnell H	Forman T	Martin F	Bratley PW	Birtles TJ	Boyle TW	Taylor JH	Ellis EE	Biggins FJ	Rutter A	Clegg JA	Travers JE	Arthurs G	Johnson P	Little J
League Apps	14	37	29	30	36	4	26	9	34	33	24	2	12	5	30	10	3	15	15	24	5	14	1	6
Goals					1		3	1	11	14	4	1		1	2	5		2	5			2		
FA Cup Apps	0	2	2	2	2	0	2	0	2	2	2	0	0	0	2	1	0	1	0	2	0	0	0	0
Goals									1						1									

PART FIVE

LIFTING THE CUP

1 Before the start of the Cup run

In the close season Manager Arthur Fairclough was allowed to bring in four players, although only Archie Taylor, a Scottish full-back signed from Huddersfield Town made the starting line-up for the opening match. Ironically for Taylor the game saw Barnsley slip to defeat at the Terriers by two goals to one. There was relief therefore when the next three matches were all won, with another of the newcomers Ron Cornoch scoring three times. Despite this there were little more than 3,000 at Oakwell for the following home game to witness a poor performance and a 2-1 defeat to Hull City. The match also marked the final appearance in the Barnsley colours for centre-half and skipper Tommy Boyle who was sold, much to the indignation of many supporters, to fellow Second Division side Burnley.

His replacement was another of the new players, Ernest Hanlon, but after he was found wanting in the task, local youngster Phil Bratley came in for his debut at home against Wolverhampton Wanderers in November. Prior to Bratleys arrival the Reds had won just once in nine games but his inclusion helped spark a mini-revival with three wins and a draw in the next four matches.

A 2-1 defeat at Chelsea had the consolation that Travers was set to return to the side and the fine form continued with three straight wins followed by two draws. This left Barnsley just four points and three places behind the Boyle-inspired Burnley who occupied the second promotion spot.

Home form was again excellent with seven wins and just a single defeat in eleven games but the difficulties of winning away were apparent with just three wins from the first six months of the season. Nevertheless, Barnsley went into the 1911-12 Cup competition with a record of six wins, three draws and just a single defeat in their previous ten matches. They were in fine form and had dispelled any fears that the league position was to be as disastrous as the previous campaign. It was perhaps too much to expect another run to the FA Cup final, but in football you just never know!

2 FA Cup First Round v Birmingham

Saturday 13 January 1912: St Andrews, Birmingham

Birmingham   0
Barnsley   0
Attendance: 18,608

When the draw for the first round of the 1912 FA Cup was made Barnsley found themselves facing Birmingham City at St Andrews. Blues were in poor form and the weekend before the Cup match went down 3-1 at home to Fulham, thus falling to 17th in the table, twelve places below their opponents who earlier in the season had won 3-1 at St Andrews.

To win Barnsley would have to find a way past Horace Peter Bailey in the home goal. Bailey had been a member of the gold medal winning Great Britain football team at the 1908 London Olympics and played most of his career as an amateur. This failed however to prevent him winning five full caps for the England side, all of them during his time at Leicester Fosse to make him the first Leicester player capped for England. Despite his undoubted skills Bailey also suffered the indignity of having to pick the ball out of the net on twelve occasions when Nottingham Forest hammered Fosse in the 1908-09 season. Bailey had joined Birmingham in 1911.

The Birmingham captain was Frank Womack, who by the time he retired in 1928 had made what remains a club record 491 league appearances and during which he failed to score even a single goal. Full-backs in 1912 and for many years afterwards rarely advanced much further than the halfway line never mind overlap as they do today. It would be interesting to know how he communicated with Albert Gardner who was profoundly deaf.

The match turned out to be poor fare to lay before the mayors of both Birmingham and Barnsley. The away side probably had the better opportunities, especially in the first half, to progress to the second round but neither side had cause for complaint when the referee blew the final whistle to signal a replay would be needed.

There was a light drizzle as the match started with Barnsley pushing forward and it didn't take long for Bailey to show what a fine keeper he was, with saves from Bartrop and Leavey being amongst his best of the first period. At the other end Cooper was rarely troubled with the *Independent* reporting that only 'Jack Kidd, Jack Hall and Billy Jones showed anything like marksmanship'.

The Barnsley half-backs were in complete control but despite their prompting the Barnsley front five were unable to push home their advantage with a goal and the away side must have left the field at half time slightly disappointed not to have scored at least once.

Urged on by Womack Birmingham stepped up the pace in the second half, Jimmy Conlin at last starting to put Glendenning and Downs under pressure. Jones should have made it 1-0 but his header from Charlie Millington's centre was wastefully wide. Lillycrop and Tufnell then failed to force Bailey into making a save from well-placed positions, and might have regretted their actions if Kidd had been able to control a bouncing ball with only Cooper to beat.

Thomas Daykin then might have done better but failed even to make the Barnsley keeper make a save with his shot from the edge of the penalty area.

The *Telegraph* felt that 'Barnsley were best represented by Cooper in goal, he gave a fine show, although he had not quite as much to do as HP Bailey, but the latter is an exceptionally brilliant custodian this year.' There was also special praise for Bratley for keeping Hall, well known as a scorer of important goals for Birmingham, in check.

Birmingham: HP Bailey, Hall, Womack [captain], Gardner, Gildea, Daykin, Millington, Jones, Hall, Kidd, Conlin

Barnsley: Cooper, Downs, Taylor, Glendenning, Bratley, Utley, Tufnell, Lillycrop, Tufnell, Travers, Leavey

The Birmingham Boss

The man in charge at Birmingham was Bob McRoberts. He was the club's first dedicated manager and had took over the reins at St Andrew's in 1910, after the club had been forced to apply for re-election to the League, remaining in charge until the outbreak of World War One. As a player, McRoberts was Chelsea's first ever £100 signing when he moved south after playing for seven seasons at Small Heath, forerunners to Birmingham.

3 FA Cup First Round Replay v Birmingham

Monday 22 January 1912: Oakwell, Barnsley

Barnsley   3   (Tufnell, Lillycrop 2)
Birmingham   0
Attendance: 12,000

There was only one change in the starting line-ups with Richard Gibson coming in for Jones in the Birmingham side. Jones or William Henry 'Billy' Jones to give him his full name was a popular player with the Birmingham fans during this time there and earned the nickname of the Tipton Smasher for scoring over a hundred goals in just over 250 appearances at the club between 1901-09 and 1912-13.

In the replay Barnsley proved far too good for a poor Birmingham side, advancing to face Leicester Fosse in round two with a goal from Tufnell and two from Lillycrop. The home side's victory would have been much more comprehensive if Bailey had not been at his best.

The first quarter of an hour saw both sides act cautiously with little in the way of scoring opportunities for either. The game broke into life courtesy of Bartrop who swept past Womack to send over a series of crosses that the Birmingham defence somehow scrambled clear. It had been rumoured in newspapers that the Birmingham captain was being considered for international honours, but despite this he had simply no answer to the Barnsley right-winger during this particular match.

It was therefore no surprise that Barnsley's opening goal on 22 minutes was the result of a raid by Bartrop whose beautiful centre was pounced upon by Lillycrop to leave Bailey with no chance. The keeper then did well to prevent a second, denying Bartrop and Tufnell with two smart saves. Lillycrop was desperately unlucky not to score his second but his powerful drive came back into play after the ball cannoned off the crossbar. Half-time came with Barnsley a goal to the good.

On 50 minutes Barnsley, watched by a decent sized crowd of 12,000 for a pre-floodlight match that kicked off on a midweek afternoon when most people would still be at work, made it two. Lillycrop pushed the ball wide to Tufnell whose powerful ground cross drive beat the keeper for pace. Bailey then dealt with shots from virtually every Barnsley forward but was powerless to prevent Lillycrop scoring his second from Leavey's centre. The home side anticipated further goals after Conlin was forced to leave the pitch but despite some good shooting opportunities the match ended with the home side winning 3-0.

The *Independent* and *Telegraph* were in no doubt who was the best player on the field – Bartrop, but there was general praise for every one of the team. In comparison only Bailey on the Birmingham side was praised for his performance.

Both newspapers were of the opinion that Barnsley would prove too strong for Leicester in the next round of the cup with the Independent reporter stating 'the Oakwell brigade promises to go far this year'.

Barnsley: Cooper, Downs, Taylor, Glendenning, Bratley, Utley, Tufnell, Lillycrop, Tufnell, Travers, Leavey

Birmingham: HP Bailey, Hall, Womack, Gardiner, Gildea, Daykin, Millington, Gibson, Hall, Kidd, Conlin

4 Off the Pitch: Robert Falcon Scott

On the day that Barnsley played Birmingham at Oakwell Robert Scott and four other Britons were experiencing the thrill of reaching the South Pole, only to be left devastated at the discovery that Roald Amundsen's Norwegian party had already beaten them by five weeks to become the first men ever to reach the South Pole.

Scott's decision not use dogs, despite the advice of expert ice travellers such as the Norwegian explorer Fridtjof Wedel-Jarlesberg Nansen, was later cited as a major factor in losing him the race to the pole and, ultimately, the lives of his party.

Plymouth-born Scott, a Royal Naval Officer who had become a popular hero after leading an expedition to the Antarctic in 1904, had marched nearly 800 miles in treacherous conditions. He was unable to disguise his anguish at coming second writing in his diary that 'All the daydreams must go, this is an awful place.'

Two days later there was nothing else to do except set off back to safety - sadly he and the four others, Edward Wilson, HR Bowers, Lawrence Oates and Edgar Evans never made it. Evans became the first to die followed by Oates on 16 March, when barely able to walk, he voluntarily left the party's tent, hoping no doubt that his sacrifice would enable the others to save themselves by walking more quickly without him. 'I am just going outside and may be some time' were recorded by Scott as Oates's last words.

With supplies running out a fierce blizzard confined the men to their tent where Scott is presumed, from the contents of his diary found later, to have been the last to die on 29 March 1912.

The three men's bodies were found by a search party on 12 November 1912 and the world was informed on 10 February 1913 along with Scott's final testimony that urged 'a great rich country like ours to see that those who are dependent on us are properly provided for'. Subsequently, the Mansion Scott Memorial Fund that was launched raised £75,000 (about £4.3 million at today's prices) to ensure dependents didn't go without.

In 1948 the film *Scott of the Antarctic* maintained the public perception of Scott as hero that has largely continued to the current day.

5 FA Cup 2nd Round v Leicester Fosse

Saturday 3 February 1912: Oakwell, Barnsley

Barnsley	1	(Lillycrop)
Leicester Fosse	0	
Attendance:	15,114	

Second Division Leicester Fosse, later to become Leicester City in 1919, arrived at Oakwell having beaten Croydon Common of the Southern League 6-1 after a replay. With Fosse having failed on twenty-one previous attempts to make it past round two the feeling was that Barnsley, lying thirteen points and eleven places higher in the table, would progress comfortably into round three. Yet whilst Barnsley did make it through they did so only because of more than a little good fortune as well as an excellent goalkeeping display by Jack Cooper. The sides had faced each other earlier in the season, Barnsley drawing 0-0 at their opponent's ground.

In light of the freezing weather then the conditions for football were always going to be tricky, and owing to a heavy downfall of snow around noon a gang of men had to be engaged to clear the pitch. In Barnsley's case it may have been better to have left things as they were as within minutes of the match getting under way those in red and white were finding it almost impossible to stay on their feet.

The West Stand at Oakwell photographed in 1912. Much of the historic building is recognisable today. Bower Collection

In contrast, the Leicester players were finding the conditions much more to their liking, and the reason was quite simple, they were wearing rubber boots, whilst Barnsley players were in their usual 'leathers'. With their footholds secure Leicester, only one win from fourteen away league and cup matches in the season so far, searched for a surprise second and piled forward from the start. Shot after shot rained down on the home goal but Cooper was in magnificent form with one save according to the *Independent* from Arthur Randle 'being masterly'. In comparison Barnsley never had even as much as a shooting opportunity in the first half and there was relief all round amongst the 15,113 crowd, that paid receipts of £493, when the referee blew his whistle for half-time at 0-0.

If the Barnsley followers hoped for better things in the second period they were rudely awakened when shortly after the teams returned to the field the Leicester left winger Willie Bauchop centred and with centre forward Willie King turning to shoot he was bundled over from behind by Bratley. Penalty and Leicester Fosse and a gilt-edged opportunity to notch the goal their performance had merited.

Cooper was not going to be beaten and he thrust out his leg to save Sam Currie's shot and when the left full-back placed the rebound wide of the post the crowd let out an almighty roar mixed with relief and celebration.

Barnsley, at last, then had a shot themselves with the ex-Barnsley man Fred Mearns saving a decent Lillycrop effort. Then, on 60 minutes, the home side took an undeserved lead when a right-wing attack involving Bartrop and Tufnell created a shooting opportunity for the former and when his shot was spilled by the keeper Lillycrop following up pushed home to make it 1-0. The soaking wet crowd couldn't believe it but it could easily have then become two nil if Mearns, partly atoning for his earlier mistake, hadn't produced a thrilling save to deny Lillycrop a second. Leicester had clearly been deflated by the Barnsley goal and although they continued to enjoy the majority of possession they managed to create only one real opportunity after that when Bauchop fired narrowly wide.

The *Independent* and *Telegraph* were afterwards full of praise for the Leicester side, with the latter making Willie King the best forward on he pitch, with Freddie Osborn and Tommy Benfield not too far behind, whilst Percy Hanger and Teddy King were rated the better backs. However, in the end it's goals that count and as Barnsley scored the only one then they went through to the next round. Most cup-winning teams rely on a little luck along the way and in 1912 there was no doubt in Barnsley's case it occurred on 3 February when Leicester Fosse came to south Yorkshire.

Barnsley: Cooper, Downs, Taylor, Glendenning, Bratley, Utley, Bartrop, Tufnell, Lillycrop, Travers, Leavey

Leicester Fosse: Mearns, Clay, Currie, Randle, Hanger, E King, Benfield, Osborn, W King, Hubbard, Bauchop

6 Home International Championships

The Home International Championship was football's oldest international series, and had been contested annually between England, Scotland, Wales and all Ireland (later Northern Ireland following independence in the south in the 1920s) since 1883-84.

Scotland won the first series and it wasn't until 1887-88 that England replaced them as winners. Wales notched their first championship in 1906-07, but at the start of the 1910 championship Ireland had yet to register their first success. (They were to do so in 1914.)

Scotland were to emerge victorious in 1910, victory by two goals to nil at Hampden Park in the final match against England proving decisive. First-half goals from James McMenemy and James Quinn sent a massive crowd of 106,205 home happy. England's team contained two players who lined up against Barnsley during the 1910 FA Cup in Jesse Pennington of WBA and Joseph Makepeace of Everton. Making his 29th international appearance was Blackburn Rovers full-back and greatest ever player Robert Crompton who was to go on to record a then record number of international caps in forty-one before World War One hostilities brought his international career to a premature end. The Arsenal and Sunderland legend Charles Buchan, writing in the 1950s, called Crompton 'the greatest ever pre-World War One footballer'.

The 1911 tournament was to be shared after England and Scotland drew 1-1 at Goodison Park before a crowd of 38,000 to give both countries five points at a time of two points for a win. England looked odds on to win but with only two minutes remaining Alexander Higgins forced the equaliser past the Middlesbrough keeper Reginald Williamson.

Both sides also finished with five points in the year when Barnsley captured the FA Cup. Having won 6-1 at Dalymount Park against Ireland and 2-0 at the Racecourse Ground, Wrexham England were in confident mood when they faced Scotland. However, they fell behind to an early Andrew Wilson goal after 7 minutes. Sunderland's George Holley crashed home the equaliser just six minutes later but try as they might after that England could not grab a winner in a match refereed by James Mason from England. You couldn't see that happening these days! The match was watched by a then world record crowd of 127,307, a figure later broken by the match on 17 April 1937 between the same sides when 149,547 packed Hampden Park. This is a figure which remains the largest ever for a match in Europe, but was subsequently overtaken as the largest crowd ever in July 1950 when 199,850 saw Brazil lose to Uruguay at the Maracana Stadium in Rio de Janeiro in the final match of the 1950 World Cup tournament.

The Home Championship came to an end in 1984 when both England and Scotland announced their withdrawal from future competitions, citing waning interest, crowded international fixture lists and the hooliganism that increasingly accompanied many of the games. With each side taking three points from a record of won one, drawn one and lost one Northern Ireland took the final championship on goal difference. Since 1984 there have been a number of attempts to revive the tournament but the English FA have made clear they have no intention of entering a team, making the idea redundant.

7 FA Cup 3rd Round v Bolton Wanderers

Saturday 24 February 1912: Burnden Park, Bolton

Bolton Wanderers	1	(Smith, 67)
Barnsley	2	(Lillycrop, 46; Leavey, 53)
Attendance:	34,598	

In light of the fact that Bolton, eighth in Division 1, had won twelve and lost just one of their previous thirteen league and cup matches at Burnden Park then few outsiders could have rated Barnsley's chances before kick-off. There was also the fact that the South Yorkshire side, sixth in Division II, had won only three of their previous fifteen away league and cup games. Bolton also had 'cup history' on their side having won through on two previous occasions to the final itself.

Yet Barnsley might well have won this third-round match rather more easily than the scoreline indicates, but were guilty of relaxing their guard after going 2-0 up in the 53rd minute and would have paid the penalty in the form of a replay if not for some wayward shooting from the Bolton forwards.

It being a cup match, the Barnsley's players had the benefit of a week's training at Lytham St Anne's, just outside Blackpool, under the direction of Will Norman, the trainer, and Mr Fairclough, secretary/manager. Bartrop's damaged shoulder had recovered to allow him to take his place in the starting line-up against a Bolton side with Jimmy Fay at centre-half.

The first half was a no-holds-barred cup contest with the pace in the first 15 minutes electric. Barnsley were grateful to rely on some smart saves by Cooper in goal, but there was also an element of luck about the Barnsley custodian's save from Jack Feebury as the ball squirmed through his hands and away from the onrushing Bolton forwards. Alf Bentley then fired over when well placed before Joe Smith heavily charged Cooper in an incident that would today produce a free kick for the keeper and very likely a booking for the attacker.

Barnsley, too, had their chances with Bartrop regularly creating shooting opportunities for this fellow forwards and although the Independent does not make clear who was involved its match report noted that in the first half 'Edmondson, in goal, made a couple of saves bordering on the miraculous, though he should have been beaten on other occasions with great chances near his goal.'

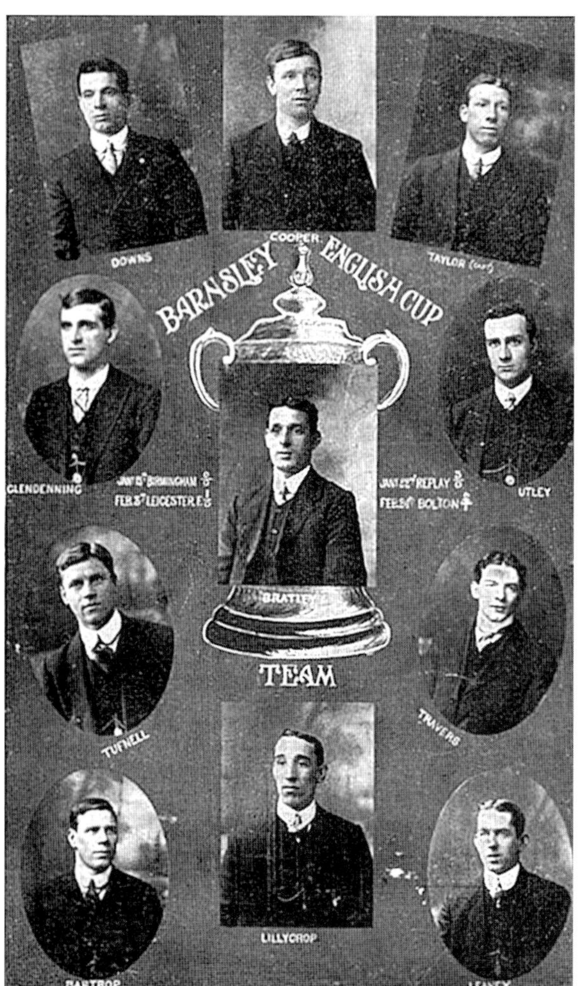

The half ended 0-0, enough to give the couple of thousand enthusiastic followers from south Yorkshire the confidence to believe their side was in with a more than decent chance of recording a famous victory. This belief was given renewed heart within a minute of the match restarting when Barnsley swept into the lead. Raiding down the left wing Leavey first saw his cross kicked clear but when he whipped a second back in Lillycrop was first to react by cracking a shot past John Edmondson.

Stung by going behind Wanderers pushed forward but were stunned when Barnsley scored their second after 53 minutes. Again Leavey was involved, his run into the box bringing Edmundson out to try to push him wide, the keeper making the fatal mistake of leaving his near post unguarded and although the

The 1911-12 Barnsley cup team looking smart in their best suits. Bower Collection angle was acute the Barnsley wing man was not to be denied and fired an accurate shot that the back-peddling Ernie Whiteside could only help up into the roof of the net. The Barnsley fans in the 34,598 crowd were overjoyed.

There was a feeling amongst the *Telegraph* and *Independent* reporters at the match that Barnsley thought that they had at this point already done enough to win the game and the side were accused of dropping back to maintain their two-goal lead.

However, any side with the quality of Joe Smith and Ted 'Wizzard' Vizard on the left flank was always in with a chance. And it was a move between these two that saw the lead halved in the 67th minute after Smith fired past Cooper and after that Barnsley relied a little too much on luck to ever leave their supporters confident of victory.

Nevertheless, when Mr Peers the referee from Liverpool blew the final whistle the result was probably just about right and Barnsley were through to the FA Cup quarter finals for the third time in their history and all in the last six years.

There was particular praise in the newspapers for Glendenning for having kept Smith and Vizard quiet for so much of the match and for Bartrop's constant menace to the home defence. But it was the team as a whole that drew the plaudits with the *Independent* stating 'Barnsley had been a solid side' and the *Telegraph* stating 'as well as skill Barnsley brought undoubted strength and stamina to the match'.

Bolton: Edmundson, Baverstock, Feebury, Barber, Fay, Whiteside, Stokes, Hogan, Bentley, Smith, Vizard

Barnsley: Cooper, Downs, Taylor (captain), Glendenning, Bratley, Utley, Bartrop, Tufnell, Lillycrop, Travers, Leavey

Bolton Wanderers

Edward 'Ted' Vizard had signed for Bolton in September 1910 from Barry Town. He went on to make over 500 appearances at outside-left before retiring as a player in 1931 after appearing in all three of the Wanderers' victorious FA Cup Final sides in 1923, 1926 and 1929. Vizard also won twenty-two international caps for Wales. He later managed Swindon Town, QPR and Wolverhampton Wanderers.

Joseph 'Joe' Smith spent almost his entire playing career with Bolton Wanderers, making his debut in 1908 and playing either as an inside or centre-forward until 1927 when he moved on to Stockport County. With 243 First

Division League goals in 410 matches he is currently tenth in the list of England's top-flight goal scorers. Together with Ted Vizard he formed a fine left flank partnership that helped Bolton reach and win two FA Cup finals in 1923 and 1926. Smith also made five international appearances for England. When he moved into management Smith's finest achievement came when he led Blackpool to victory at Wembley in the 1953 FA Cup final, where ironically the defeated finalists were none other than Bolton Wanderers.

The Bolton Wanderers manager was Will Settle who served in that capacity from 1910 till 1915. He was successful in taking the side to promotion into the First Division at the end of the 1910-11 season.

9 FA Cup 4th Round v Bradford City

Saturday 9 March 1912: Oakwell, Barnsley

Barnsley   0
Bradford City 0
Attendance: 24,987

Victory against Bolton saw Barnsley 'rewarded' with a home tie against the cup holders, Bradford City. The side from Valley Parade had surprised the football world by beating holders Newcastle United after a replay at Old Trafford in April 1911, Albert Speirs striking the only goal of the game, after 15

The cup-holders Bradford City prior to their 4th round FA Cup game at Oakwell, 9 March 1912. Bower Collection

minutes. Speirs, one of eight Scots in the Bradford team, later died on active service, being killed during the Battle of Passchendaele in August 1917, aged 31.

In rounds one and two of the 1912 competition Bradford City had put out QPR, after a replay, and their near neighbours Chelsea - three games in which they failed to concede a goal. Then in Round 3 they squeezed past near neighbours Bradford Park Avenue, winning 1-0. In fact since 14 January 1911 Bradford City had played twelve games in the English Cup competition, scoring sixteen goals, whilst conceding just one - against Norwich City in the second round of 1911. Clearly if Barnsley were to emulate their near neighbours the breaking down of their defence would be key, especially at home where they enjoyed the best chance of success. To do so they would have to break past Robert Campbell, one of the Bradford backs and most able players of the time.

Barnsley had declared in print their confidence of knocking out the cup holders and with the wind behind them in the first half they pressed from the start, causing Campbell initially to lose his customary calm. This allowed the Barnsley forwards, with Leavey and Bartrop dashing past the half backs, to make and miss one or two decent scoring opportunities. An early goal would have totally changed the nature of the competitive affair but Campbell gradually asserted his greatness as a footballer by his constant interceptions when danger threatened, so Mark Mellors in goal was well protected. At half-time the feeling amongst the crowd appears from contemporary reports to have been that Barnsley had missed their chance - especially as Bradford City would be kicking with the wind in the second half.

And so it seemed initially when the away side took the game to the Tykes but the most Cooper was asked to do was collect a poor Devine header before the rhythm of the first half returned with Barnsley attacking and the Bradford defence steadfastly resisting their advances. So devoid were the cup holders of attacking intent that Downs, the Barnsley full-back, abandoned his defensive duties and piled forward in support of his colleagues in attack. Travers was only inches away from a Bartrop cross and Leavey should probably have done better with a straight shot that Mellors collected comfortably. Downs then made a dashing run with the ball and with nothing coming their way the Bradford forwards, with the exception of outside right Dicky Bond, all began dropping back to help out in defence. Yet the England international winger might have given the away side the lead as, getting the ball just inside his half, he beat Taylor and raced down on goal. As he moved towards the penalty area the Barnsley defender cynically took him down. Today of course it would be a sending-off but not so almost a century ago and the free-kick proved to be the last chance Bradford had to win the match as after that it was all Barnsley.

Utley had a shot saved by Mellors who later on in life went on to become a successful businessman in the wool trade. Glendenning then found Bartrop, whose shot was blocked but try as Barnsley did the magnificent Bradford defence would not yield and the match ended 0-0.

The *Telegraph's* 'Looker On' particularly praised Leavey in his match report remarking that Liverpool had been foolish to let him leave. He also felt that the Barnsley forwards may have been affected by the occasion, and felt that they would have to play better if the side were to progress to the next round. It was clear, especially in light of their tremendous home record in the FA Cup since they had first entered in 1903, that Bradford were now the favourites but Looker On felt 'that if the Bradford forwards proved as hapless at Valley Parade as they did at Oakwell I would not be surprised if the result after 90 minutes was another goalless draw, and if extra-time has to be played then the odds are very great in Barnsley's favour'.

With Irvine Boocock having broken a small bone in his ankle in the last minute of the match Bradford would need to make at least one change for the replay game on the Wednesday.

Barnsley: Cooper, Downs, Taylor, Glendenning, Bratley, Utley, Bartrop, Tufnell, Lillycrop, Travers, Leavey

Bradford City: Mellors, Campbell, Boocock, Robinson, Torrance, McDonald, Bond, Speirs, O'Rourke, Devine, Logan

10 FA Cup 4th Round Replay v Bradford City

Wednesday 13 March 1912 : Valley Parade, Bradford

Bradford City 0
Barnsley   0
Attendance: 31,910

Both teams lived to fight another day in a match that thrilled a crowd of 31,910 who paid £1,267 to see who might progress to the FA Cup semi-finals. Although Barnsley were again the better side Bradford played much better than in the first match at Oakwell although they again relied heavily on their magnificent defence in which Bob Torrance was outstanding and Campbell and Bert Gane played fine games. As the busier keeper by far, Mellors also emerged with great credit and was probably the man most responsible for ensuring the match ended all square.

Barnsley down the left with Leavey and Travers were a constant menace, the two interlinking to create opportunities for themselves and the other Barnsley forwards but it seemed that once again they all were a little intimidated by the occasion when presented with the chance to score the winning goal.

It was the home side that showed first with Bond providing a decent heading opportunity that Frank Thompson failed to head powerfully enough to beat Cooper. After that Barnsley looked to make the decisive opening with Glendenning, Utley and Bratley bringing the ball forward to give their attacking colleagues a chance to show their skills. Mellors made a glorious save to deny Tufnell and the sides left the pitch at half-time level at 0-0.

The second period began with Barnsley again moving forward, but there was a danger of being caught on the counter attack and so it almost proved when Thompson provided a wonderful cross to an unmarked Peter Logan who failed to connect with no one near him. Still Barnsley pressed, but Lillycrop at centre forward was constantly blotted out by Torrance and as cross after cross floated in Mellors came out to collect confidently. Leavey seemed to have beaten the keeper just before the end of normal time but the ball passed the post by the nearest of margins.

Extra-time proved a frenetic, strenuous affair in which two teams battled heroically on a muddy pitch to try to force a winner, whilst being determined not to concede a goal themselves. Mellors provided the most dramatic moment when scrambling across the goal to magnificently push clear a Leavey shot that threatened to enter his goal at the far corner. His momentum took him crashing into the post and crashing down onto the turf. Trainers and soon a doctor all appeared and after he was revived the keeper refused to take their advice and insisted on bravely playing on. Fortunately for him Barnsley were too exhausted to put him under pressure for the remaining 22 minutes of extra-time and at the end the crowd gave him a hero's reception for his pluck. When the referee sounded the final whistle the game had ended 0-0 and the teams were set to repeat the affair the following Monday at Elland Road, Leeds. It threatened to be a tense affair to see who would win through to face Swindon Town in the 1912 FA Cup semi-final.

Bradford City: Mellors, Campbell, Gane, Robinson, Torrance, McDonald, Bond, Logan, O'Rourke, Devine, Thompson

Barnsley: Cooper, Downs, Taylor, Glendenning, Bratley, Utley, Bartrop, Tufnell, Lillycrop, Travers, Leavey

11 Off the Pitch: Miners' Strike in 1912

1 March 1912 signalled the start of what was then the biggest disputes in British trade union history when 800,000 coal miners came out under the direction of the Miners' Federation of Great Britain (MFGB), the first truly national miners' union.

The strike was the culmination of determined and continuous agitation for a minimum wage in the preceding years. This was obstinately refused by mine owners on the grounds that it would mean men would be 'shirking' instead of performing the tasks they were paid for. In February 1912 the MFGB balloted members who voted 445,801 for strike action with 115,921 against.

With coal then, of course, absolutely vital to the economy the Government was determined to do everything possible to prevent a strike and urged without success both sides to compromise. Despite the meagre strike pay and great privation in every coalfield the strike was rock solid leading to factories being forced on to short-time working and train services everywhere being cut.

As coal was the sole means of domestic and institutional heating, shortages soon led to severe problems, forcing the Government to call the two sides together on 12, 13 and 14 March and a Parliamentary Bill conceding the principle of a minimum wage, but to the miners' dismay no actual figures, was introduced on 19 March.

Striking miners outcropping for coal in Barnsley during the 1912 strike. Wood Collection

Miners were hoping for a minimum weekly wage of not less than 5s (25p or about £14.30 in today's money) for all adult workers, and 2s [10p] a day for boys at fourteen and although they voted 244,011 to continue against 201,013 to go back a special MFGB delegates conference agreed (although those from Yorkshire and Lancashire were opposed) to return to work as fewer than two-thirds were in favour of staying out.

The miners felt they had been tricked by the Government and returned to work bitterly disappointed but it could be said, in hindsight, that the miners' were now a powerful and united fighting force, and that their experience at the hands of the Liberal government consolidated the conviction that the working class must have its own, independent political party - hardly surprising therefore that by 1922 Barnsley moved to support the Labour Party at the General Election.

12 FA Cup 4th Round 2nd Replay v Bradford City

Monday 18 March 1912: Elland Road, Leeds

Barnsley   0
Bradford City 0
Attendance: 37,000

The sheer numbers of people wanting to watch this fourth-round match second replay overwhelmed the ground and the surrounding areas and it was a miracle that in the circumstances no-one was killed, especially in light of the fact that the authorities had forgotten to ensure that at least one ambulance was on hand for all eventualities. Although the gates were not due to be opened until 1.00pm a large crowd had already assembled by noon and at 12.05 pm thousands rushed the gates with little the handful of police on duty could do to stop many spectators gaining free entry. Whether those involved had turned up intent on gaining free entry or had just spotted an opportunity to do so cannot be known but it is a fact that money had never been harder to come by in Barnsley, and in other parts of Yorkshire, due to the continuing strike in the coal mines.

Thus it was that by the time the game kicked off the ground was absolutely packed, with thousands outside, many of whom had taken to climbing on the roofs of nearby houses, shops and factories. Thousands desperate for even the remote chance of witnessing the winning goal populated a slagheap around a third of a mile from the ground.

It had proved necessary for the police to use horses to control the crowd

George Travers, Dickie Downs, Will Norman, Jackie Cooper, George Utley and Archie Taylor photographed at the Pontefract Road end goal in 1912. Wood Collection

Several of the Barnsley team 'in training' during the 1912 cup campaign. Wood Collection

Harry Tufnell, Phil Bratley and George Lillycrop in front of the West Stand take time out from a training session in 1912. Wood Collection

inside the ground, and for much of the game they actually patrolled from inside the playing area pushing back the crowd each time it spilled on to the pitch. Eventually it proved too much and the referee abandoned the game with ten minutes remaining. In truth it should never have been started, but with such a large passionate crowd already assembled the authorities must have feared a riot if the game hadn't gone ahead. Not that the end of the game ended the mayhem, because in the aftermath the takings box was ransacked and a large sum of money taken. No-one, it appears, was ever caught or convicted of the offence.

In the circumstances it would have been extremely difficult for either side to have played anything like their best, especially as in Barnsley's case they lost Leavey after 25 minutes with a double break to his leg, the outside-left being carried from the field by a great body of spectators and somehow taken to hospital. Yet even with ten men the Second Division side always seemed to be the most likely to open the scoring and Gane made a great interception to deny Lillycrop as half-time approached to keep the scores level. Logan provided Archie Devine with a great opportunity with just seconds remaining but Cooper was in fine form, making a good stop.

When the second period got under way Lillycrop was prominent in attack and Mellors was forced to get down low to block his shot. Barnsley then forced two corners and then Glendenning was only foiled by another decent Mellors save as the ten men pressed for the opening goal of the match and tie.

Bradford seemed certain to take the lead when Harold Walden was clean through but Cooper, showing great judgement, came out quickly to boot the ball to safety. The keeper should however have had no chance in the next attack but Bond somehow conspired to roll the ball wide when presented with an open goal from just eight yards out, the crowd spilling on to the pitch in their anxiety to see if the ball had entered the goal and holding up the game for many minutes afterwards.

When play did resume both teams seemed determined to grab the winner and both keepers had to be alert to a succession of dangerous crosses and hard hit shots, before Lillycrop, receiving a lovely pass from Tufnell, missed the sort of chance that the normally reliable attacker would have gobbled up. With each attack the crowd grew ever more excited and as the match moved towards its end more and more encroachments on to the pitch occurred, with the referee continuously halting the game to allow the police to move spectators off the playing area. However, with ten minutes left, when various parts of the ground were overwhelmed by spectators, the referee decided it was no longer possible to continue and abandoned the game.

Bradford City: Mellors, Campbell, Gane, Hampton, Torrance, McDonald, Bond, Fox, Walden, Devine, Logan

Barnsley: Cooper, Downs, Taylor, Glendenning, Bratley, Utley, Bartrop, Tufnell Lillycrop, Travers, Leavey

13 FA Cup 4th Round 3rd Replay v Bradford City

Thursday 21 March 1912: Bramall Lane, Sheffield

Barnsley	3	(Travers, Lillycrop 2)
Bradford City	2	(Speirs, Devine)
Attendance:	38,264	

Match report taken from *Barnsley Independent* of 21.03.1912:

How the cup holders were conquered

Dramatic Finish

By 'Centre-forward'

A truly great cup-tie was that wherein the Barnsley and Bradford City teams meeting yesterday for the fourth time in the fourth round of the English Cup competition at Bramall Lane succeeded in settling the question of supremacy. It would be difficult to imagine a more thrilling and exciting struggle or one where wherein fortune fluctuated more greatly. From the first moment to the last, the vast crowd that gathered in the Sheffield United enclosure was kept keenly interested as first one side and then the other gained the upper hand until absolutely the last kick of a spirited stirring struggle Barnsley passed into the semi-final. After playing previous games for nearly five hours without scoring a goal these Yorkshire rivals yesterday scored five, three of them went to Barnsley who will go to Chelsea to play Swindon en route to the Palace. The heroes of Oakwell gained the lead, lost it, but made a splendid recovery and finally right on the call of time scored a sensational winning goal. We have had many thrilling finishes in cup-ties at Sheffield but none more thrilling than this.

The better team
In winning by the odd goal in five Barnsley had their desserts. To this extent they were the superior team. Equal to the Cup holders in defence they were speedier

and smarter in the manner of finishing their attacks, and the score was a fair indication of the character of the players and the merits of the contending teams. Whilst both played well in defence there was a decided improvement in the form of both sets of forwards on what had been seen in previous games. Chances of course were missed by both but all the same some very fine shots were sent in - the improvement was especially noticeable on the part of Bradford City who during the earlier part of the game gave Cooper several shots to deal with and which he would have been forgiven for missing. They were beaten by a slightly better team so in that sense they were a little unlucky to lose for twice during the first half of the game did a great shot rattle the Barnsley bar with the goalkeeper completely beaten.

Successful experiment
With Leavey, who unhappily broke his leg in last Monday's game at Leeds, of course not available the Barnsley committee tried the bold experiment of playing Moore, a right winger, in the position of outside left. The experiment was an unqualified success, the willing reserve showing speed, skill, accuracy and strength in shooting and was fearless in his way of facing the burly Campbell. Another feature of the Barnsley forwards was the excellent display given by Lillycrop who led the line with good judgement, passed and shot well, was dashing and bold and was responsible for the equalising and then finally the winning goal. The Bradford City committee recognising where there weakness lay in the previous contests re-arranged their forward line, leaving out Bond and Oscar Fox who played at Leeds, bringing in Jimmy Speirs and Thompson and moving the versatile Logan from the outside left to the outside right. Whatever may be thought of the wisdom of leaving out Bond certain it is that the line as a whole played better than the previous time and though they did not always finish their attacks strongly some of their shots especially from Devine, Speirs and Thompson were admirable and Cooper was taxed to the limit to stop their furious drives.

Barnsley's Start
Barnsley opened the scoring 15 minutes from the start, Travers, with a fierce low shot flashing the ball just inside the post as Mellors vainly made a desperate effort to reach it. From a centre by Bartrop, Lillycrop with a beautiful shot was within an ace of scoring again, and a little later he gave Travers a glorious chance of doing so, but, unhampered, favourably placed with plenty of time and plenty of room, the inside left lifted the ball over the bar. Before Barnsley had scored James McDonald was very unfortunate with a fine shot which beat Cooper and hit the angle of the goalposts, and afterwards Thompson was equally unlucky in not equalising with an exactly similar effort, but on the general form displayed the men from Oakwell deserved their lead of a goal.

Bradford's response

Space will not allow me to mention one half the thrilling incidents of the second half. Beginning indifferently the City improved, and twenty minutes after change of ends a well placed corner kick by Thompson enabled Speirs to head an equaliser. Ten minutes later Devine, taking a pass from the right, tricked Downs and giving Cooper no chance with a fine shot to put the cup holders ahead. Barnsley then seemed to lose their dash, but they awoke to a great effort with time drawing near, and when with only five minutes to go a corner kick followed by a scrimmage in front ended in Lillycrop heading an equalising goal the great crowd went wild with excitement and enthusiasm. The last few minutes of the 90 were thrilling, as Lillycrop hit the Bradford bar and Thompson the Barnsley upright.

The winning goal

With the score two goals each extra-time was played, and on heavy ground the well trained teams kept up the pace wonderfully well. First one side and then the other vainly attacked, and we were all preparing for another replay when the final sensation came to startle us. In the last half minute Barnsley made one last desperate burst. Bartrop drove the ball in and Mellors beat it out, Glendenning sent it across to Lillycrop who hooked it into the net as Mellors, who had scarcely recovered from his previous save vainly threw himself at it. Lillycrop seemed at first scarcely to know what had happened but when he realised that he had scored the winning goal he danced with delight until smothered by his joyous comrades. This was the last kick of the match, for before the ball could be placed in the centre of the field again the referee sounded time. Barnsley had beaten the Cup holders and their friends went home rejoicing.

The gate

I must confess that I was surprised to learn the official figure. Looking round the vast assemblage before the match it seemed to me the biggest crowd that during a long experience I had even seen at Bramall Lane and I expected to lean that the record had been broken, that something like 45,000 were present. But it was not so, for the number of people paying for admission was 38,241 and the receipts £1394 16s 4d. There have been two bigger crowds than yesterday's at Bramall Lane, namely three years ago at the semi-final between Newcastle United and Manchester United when 49,118 paid and at a league game between Sheffield United and Newcastle last New Year's Day when between 42-43,000 people were present.

Barnsley: Cooper, Downs, Taylor, Glendenning, Bratley, Utley, Bartrop, Tufnell, Lillycrop, Travers, Moore

Bradford City: Mellors, Campbell, Gane, Hampton, Torrance, McDonald, Logan, Spiers, Walden, Devine, Thompson

Incidently, when George Travers scored in the 15th minute he broke an FA Cup record that still stands to this day. Bradford City were the FA Cup holders and in the previous twelve cup games spanning the 1910-11 and 1911-12 seasons they had not conceded a goal.

From the *Barnsley Independent*, 21.03.1912:

Snow, slush, together with rain many times repeated were not sufficient to dampen the enthusiasm of hundreds of football fans who tramped over from the Barnsley district for sheer necessity propelled the use of 'Shank's mare' as owing to the coal war the train service is almost hopelessly disorganised and from the same cause the bulk of these enthusiasts had not money with which to pay for a train service.

Soon after nine o'clock, writes an independent representative, little groups of men and youths were to be seen near Wentworth station plodding citywards. They had suffered an hour's snowstorm, which had clothed the roads and countryside in white, and looked wretched but resolute.

Gradually the struggling procession increased, the enthusiasts coming along in ones, twos and threes and occasionally in dozens. But they followed each other in quick procession, and after several hours added animation to the sloppy turnpike which otherwise would have been almost deserted. Many of the travellers, a number of the them 'pitlads' had neither overcoat or 'mack', they made no mystery of the fact they were already wet through and accordingly it was anything but a triumphal procession - but to turn back? They scorned the suggestion. When opportunity offered some of the more active spirits tried to rouse the spirits by singing for 'good old Bairnsla!' But for the most part they plodded and plodded with the skies seeming to frown all the while, mentally counting for the last milestone which would bring them into the great city. All their energy was concentrated on 'getting there' since a good proportion of them were making their first acquaintance with the road. One group lightened the monotony of the journey with a noisy clatter of rattles, whilst other men got inspiration from a melancholy cornet and band bells.

Trampers from Bradford
One party were fortunate in commandeering the goodwill of the drivers of a big

brewery motor and perched on the top of numerous 36-gallon casks they made great sport of their foot sore comrades who tried to keep a brave heart in face of adversity. A number of the lucky passengers hailed from Bradford. As a matter of fact, many supporters from the woollen town tramped all the way, but half of the journey was done on the Wednesday. The Barnsley enthusiasts came from places as widely apart as Hemsworth, Ryhill, Staincross, Dodworth, Barnsley, Worsbro', Hoyland and Wombwell.

Several hundred colliers in clogs must have passed me on the road during the four hours. Often they looked limp and stiff, and suggested a problem of 'what about the return journey?' There is not the least room for doubt that many of the enthusiasts had not more than the price of admission to the ground.

The Last Copper
This was strongly borne out by the fact that they were not able to avail themselves of the boon of a penny train ride when the outskirts of the city was reached. Many who had intended to make the trip abandoned it at the last minute owing to the weather.

A singular fact is that many of the trampers went by strange round about routes to get to the city. Some turned off at Harley and went via Rotherham; others went on to the Wortley road and travelled via Greneside and Wadsley Bridge, and more strange of all, at Ecclesfield not a few left the straight route to the city and went three miles out of their way through Southey and into the city via Owlerton.

14 FA Cup Semi-Final v Swindon Town

Saturday 30 March 1912: Stamford Bridge, London

Barnsley	0
Swindon Town	0

Attendance:	48,057

Barnsley's reward for knocking out the cup holders Bradford City after a titanic four-match struggle was to play Swindon Town of the Southern League. The teams had clashed once before in the FA Cup, when back in 1902-03 the Tykes had triumphed 4-0 in the final qualifying round before the first round proper. Considering that the other semi-final was between First Division

1911 Cup portraits of the 'Battling Barnsley' the 'Hope of Yorkshire'. Note the little mascot (young Sammy) on his bike. Bower Collection

Front of the Chelsea programme for the 1912 Barnsley v Swindon FA Cup Semi-final at Stamford Bridge featured a cartoon of the contest. Wood Collection

THE "MINERS" ATTEMPT TO WRECK THE HOPE OF THE SOUTH.

Barnsley (The Miner): "If I can switch him on t'other line, he'll stop right enough."

leaders, and eventual winners, Blackburn Rovers and another First division side in West Bromwich Albion, there was little doubt that Barnsley had enjoyed a fortunate draw. Not that Swindon would be a walkover as just two years previously they'd lost out on a place in the final by losing at the semi-final stage at White Hart Lane to Barnsley's cup final conquerors Newcastle United.

Swindon had knocked out First Division Notts County and Everton and two non-League sides, West Ham United and Sutton Junction en route to the semi-final. The side's star man was inside forward Harold Fleming, recent scorer of a hat-trick during a 6-1 England win in Dublin against Ireland, who went on to become a club legend by scoring over 200 goals in just over 300 matches in a career shortened by the World War I during which he was a physical education instructor.

Fleming also played eleven times for England before the war, scoring an impressive nine times and proving so popular that he even had a style of boot named after him during his career. A statue of Fleming stands in the County Ground's foyer today and there is even a road named after him close by.

Swindon's second inside forward was Archie Bown who had scored the quarter- final winner against Everton and although his was another career shortened by the carnage of 1914-18 his 125 goals for the Wiltshire club means he remains their fifth highest goalscorer ever.

With no team from the south having reached the FA Cup final since Southampton in 1902, the match aroused extraordinary interest in that part of England, and thousands were left disappointed at being unable to gain entry when the gates were closed in the run-up to kick-off. In truth those who missed out didn't miss much as the game was never a classic, with Swindon if anything enjoying the best of the action. A strong wind blowing straight down the ground couldn't have helped but it appeared that the whole occasion had got to many of the players, with defenders in particular unwilling to risk a mistake and settling for a good old fashioned boot it anywhere when it came near them. Barnsley were also criticised in the following day's papers for their willingness to employ rough tactics in order to prevent the Swindon forwards, and Fleming in particular, fashioning an opening for a shot at goal. On two or three occasions Swindon players were forced to take a breather from the action after a strong challenge.

It was down the left with Bown and Lamb where the Southern League side showed the greatest likelihood of breaking through in the first half, but Glendenning was in fine form and he and Downs slowly established a stranglehold on their opponents. Harry Kay, unusually for the time, coming forward from full-back, was clever enough to use the wind to force Cooper into making the first real save of the match. Bown should have opened the scoring but his header from just six yards flew over with Cooper beaten. Bob Jefferson was then unlucky when his shot beat the keeper but the ball landed on the top of the net rather than inside it, to the relief of the Barnsley followers. Just before the break Barnsley at last threatened but just as Lillycrop manoeuvred to shoot he was squeezed out by the combined efforts of Billy Silto and Jock Walker. The Barnsley man was then denied by a good Skillar save but when the loose ball ran to Tufnell it seemed that with an open goal beckoning Barnsley must take the lead, yet Tufnell appeared terrified and somehow managed to hit the ball so that it actually flew out for a throw-in on the far side of the pitch.

The second half also saw Travers miss for Barnsley when well placed, whilst Len Skiller made a fine save from a Bartrop free-kick whilst at the opposite end Jefferson was unable to control the ball when left with only Cooper to beat. Fleming, who had been very quiet, was then in action as first Downs and then Taylor checked his darting runs before Cooper punched away a Lamb cross and made a decent save from Fleming.

The match ended 0-0, and meant the teams would meet four days later at Notts County to see who would play either Blackburn or WBA, whose game also finished 0-0, in the final.

Swindon: Skillar, Kay, Walker, Handley, Silto, Chambers, Jefferson, Fleming, Wheatcroft, Bown, Lamb

Barnsley: Cooper, Downs, Taylor, Glendenning, Bratley, Utley, Bartrop, Tufnell, Lillycrop, Travers, Moore

15 1912 FA Cup Semi-Final Replay v Swindon Town

Wednesday 3 April 1912: Meadow Lane, Nottingham

Barnsley	1	(Bratley)
Swindon Town	0	

Attendance	18000

Given the distances involved it was hardly surprising that Barnsley, who wore a change strip of Oxford blue in this game, enjoyed the backing of more of their followers than Swindon Town. Amongst those who made the trip were a good number who'd walked from South Yorkshire to Nottingham setting off, in many cases, on the Tuesday. Those with more money in their pockets came by train, motorcars and vans and taxi. All were ecstatic when the final whistle sounded and Barnsley had won through to their second FA Cup final in three years, where their opponents would be West Bromwich Albion, the conquerors of Blackburn Rovers by one goal to nil.

Barnsley's heroes were undoubtedly goalkeeper Cooper who kept the scores level in the first half by saving Bown's penalty, and centre-half Bratley who scored the winner after ten minutes of the second half. The result was no more than Barnsley deserved for they played much better than in the first match and were the superior team on the day. They were helped considerably by an injury to Kay after just ten minutes which reduced the Swindon back to a passenger for the rest of the game.

Much thus depended on John 'Jock' Wallace, a Scottish international back who had played his sixth international for his country on the 23 March in a 1-1 draw at Hampden Park, against England, before a then world record crowd of 127,307. Walker went on to make a total of eight appearances for his country. He was a competitive player with a strong tackle, and a good header of the ball and he was one of the finest players ever to play for Swindon Town.

Swindon had also suffered a blow before the game when Fleming was declared unable to play, Burkinshaw taking his place. Despite this, it was the Southern League side who started the brightly and penned their league opponents in their half for the first ten minutes with Cooper making a number of good catches from crosses sent in from both wings. Thankfully, Moore was able to relieve the pressure by breaking away and after that the game settled down in the first half to a much more even contest. The first real chance fell to Barnsley but Bartrop's shot from twelve yards out lacked pace, allowing Skillar to save comfortably. Utley then saw his shot crash back into play from the crossbar before Burkinshaw thought he'd given the Railwaymen the lead

A commemorative postcard of 'Little Sammy', Barnsley's young mascot in 1912.
Firth Collection

and was horribly disappointed to see his header flash also inches over the bar after the ball had beaten Cooper.

Tufnell, Lillycrop and Bratley then all brought saves from the Swindon keeper as the southern side were continuously pressed back. When they did break away Utley made a poor challenge on Jefferson to leave the referee with no option, after ignoring muted appeals for off-side, to award a penalty. Bown's shot was hard but too straight to beat Cooper who fisted the ball away, Glendenning racing in to complete the clearance to the tumultuous cheers of the Barnsley faithful. The half closed with Travers trying to shoulder charge Skillar into the net but to no great effect leaving the match all square at 0-0.

It took Barnsley only ten minutes of the second period to take the lead their supporters so desired, and it came after intense pressure in which Travers had hit the bar, Bartrop the post; and numerous crosses had been cleared by a desperate Swindon defence. The goal came when Bartrop dropped a delightful cross into the box and Bratley rose to powerfully head home, before he was literally submerged under a mass of celebrating Barnsley bodies. It may have been 1912 but they were after all only 35 minutes away from playing in the biggest football game on the planet at the time - the FA Cup final.

It was Cooper who ensured this was the case a few minutes later when he produced a truly wonderful save by twisting to turn Jefferson's shot over the bar for a corner. Swindon seemed to wilt after this and Barnsley should really have wrapped the game up on a number of occasions with all their forwards being guilty of missing the sort of chances they could normally have been expected to gobble up. All was forgotten, however, when the referee blew the final whistle on a famous victory. Could Barnsley now go one better than in 1910 and win the FA Cup for the first time in the club's history?

Barnsley: Cooper, Downs, Taylor, Glendenning, Bratley, Utley, Bartrop, Tufnell, Lillycrop, Travers, Moore

Swindon: Skillar, Kay, Walker, Handley, Silto, Chambers, Jefferson, Burkinshaw, Wheatcroft, Bown, Lamb

Barnsley's cup run meant they had a number of League games to play and they played five games in eight days remarkably winning three and losing just one.

16 Off the Pitch: The *Titanic* sinks

Five days before the 1912 FA Cup final came the dreadful news that the *Titanic* had hit an iceberg on its maiden voyage and sank within three hours. As a result 1,517 people lost their lives, making it one of the most deadly peacetime maritime disasters ever.

The RMS *Titanic* was owned by the White Star Line and built at the Harland and Wolff shipyard in Belfast. With a capacity for 3,547 passengers, she was the largest passenger steamship in the world at the time of her launch on 31 May 1911.

Completed on 31 March 1912, she set sail from Southampton bound for New York on Wednesday 10 April 1912. On board were some of the most prominent people of the time. On Sunday 14 April, at 13.35, a warning from the steamer *Amerika* concerning large icebergs in the Titanic's path was not passed to the master of the ship, Captain Edward J Smith, as Jack Philips and Harold Bride, the Marconi wireless operators, were only paid to relay messages to and from passengers. Eight hours later disaster struck when a last minute sighting of an iceberg by lookouts Frederick Fleet and Reginald Lee failed to allow sufficient time to prevent a collision.

Within minutes it was clear that with five forward compartments flooding with water the ship was certain to sink and shortly after midnight the lifeboats were readied and a distress call was sent out, with the nearest ship to respond being the *Carpathia*, fifty-eight miles and four hours away.

Although it was complying with the regulations of the time, the ship did not carry enough lifeboats for everyone on board, with a capacity of just 1,178. It was clear that with 2,240 people aboard then not everyone could hope to survive and the 'women and children first' policy led to a disproportionate number of men dying. Third-class passengers also suffered considerably more than those in first class, with only 23.8% surviving compared with 60.5%. Most deaths were the result of hypothermia in the freezing water. In total, 706 passengers and crew survived, some of whom were plucked from the water by the *Carpathia* which arrived at 4.10am and left four hours later bound for New York where it arrived on 18 April.

Within days the US authorities had set up an inquiry into the cause of the disaster and all survivors were prevented from returning to England until this ended on 25 May.

Back in Britain the public demanded answers themselves. The *Titanic* was popularly believed to have been 'unsinkable' and Lord Mersey was appointed to head the inquiry that followed. This took place between 2 May and 13 July 1912. The investigations found that many safety rules were outdated and recommended new laws. As a result numerous safety improvements for ocean-going vessels were implemented including improved life-vest design, the holding of safety drills and improved radio communications.

The massive media coverage that followed the *Titanic's* sinking, the famous victims, changes in maritime law, and the eventual discovery of the wreck more than seventy-three years later, have all contributed to the continuing interest in the *Titanic*.

17 Cup Final Opponents: West Bromwich Albion

Barnsley's opponents in the 1912 FA Cup final were West Bromwich Albion. Promoted to Division 1 at the end of the previous season the Baggies had enjoyed a decent season and were lying in mid-table prior to the final with three games in hand on sides directly above them with Blackburn Rovers, their conquered semi-final opponents, set to capture the league title.

One of the founder members of the Football League in 1888, WBA were hoping to win the FA Cup for the third time after trophy success in 1888 and 1892, although there had also been disappointment with defeats at the 1886, 1887 and 1895 finals.

En route to the Crystal Palace WBA had put out three Division One sides in Blackburn, Tottenham Hotspur and Sunderland as well as two sides from Division Two in Leeds City and Fulham.

A rare souvenir napkin of the 1912 FA Cup Final at Crystal Palace.
Wood Collection

Round 1	Spurs (H) 3-0 (Bowser, Deacey, Wright)
Round 2	Leeds City (A) 1-0 (Bowser)
Round 3	Sunderland (A) 2-1 (Pailor 2)
Round 4	Fulham (H) 3-0 (Bowser, Wright)
Semi Final at Anfield	Blackburn Rovers 0-0
Semi Final Replay at Hillsborough	Blackburn 1-0 (after extra time - Pailor)

West Bromwich Albion's side in both games in the 1912 Final was as follows:

18 West Bromwich Albion Player-Profiles

Hubert Pearson (goalkeeper) was a well-built, courageous goalkeeper, who was born in Tamworth, Staffs on 15 May 1866 and died in Tamworth on 10 October 1955. He joined WBA from Tamworth Athletic in February 1906, turned professional the following month and remained with the club until his retirement in May 1926. He made 377 appearances (League and Cup) and scored two League goals, both penalties, in 1911-12 against Bury and Middlesbrough, both at home. He helped Albion win the Second Division and First Division championships (1911 and 1920 respectively), played in the 1912 FA Cup final, was an England reserve (once selected to play against France in 1925 but was forced to miss out through injury) and twice represented the Football League. His son, Harold Pearson, also a goalkeeper, joined him at the Hawthorns in April 1925.

Arthur Cook (right-back) was a solid right-back, who was born in Stafford on 14 September 1890 and died in Stafford (whilst sleep walking at his pub, The Doxey Arms) on 13 February 1930. He played for Stafford Rangers and

Wrexham before joining WBA in May 1911. He remained with the club until August 1921, making fifty-five senior appearances. He later played for Luton Town, Swansea Town and Whitchurch.

Jessie Pennington (left-back), an all-time legend and born in West Bromwich, was an elegant left-back and a peerless captain of the club. An automatic choice for nineteen years, his career was interrupted by World War One, but that didn't stop him captaining the club to their only League title in 1919-20, as well as playing in the Division Two winning team of 1910-11 and the losing FA Cup side in 1912. He played for England twenty-five times, captaining the side on occasions. Pennington returned to act as a scout for Albion from 1950 to 1960 and was made a life member of the club in 1969, a year before he died in Kidderminster. Pennington was named as one of West Bromwich Albion's sixteen greatest players in a poll organised as part of the club's 125th anniversary celebrations in 2004. Pennington made 455 league appearances for West Brom along with thirty-nine FA Cup and two other appearances.

West Brom's Jessie Pennington photographed prior to the 1912 Cup Final. Wood Collection

George Baddeley (right-half) was born in the Potteries in May 1874 and was a right-half with Burslem Swifts, Pitshill and Biddulph FC before joining Stoke as captain in 1900. He made over 200 appearances for his home town club before transferring to Albion in June 1908. He spent the next six years at The Hawthorns, helping the Baggies win the Second Division in 1911 and reach the FA Cup final the following season. He is the oldest player ever to appear in a senior game for Albion – he was almost forty when he made his 157th and final appearance for the club in April 1914. Later working in the upholstery trade, George died in West Bromwich in July 1952. At the time George Baddeley was the oldest man to play in a cup final at almost thirty-nine years of age. Only three have since beaten his record - David Seaman in 2003 with Arsenal, Charlton Athletic's John Oakes in 1946 and the oldest, Walter (Billy) Hampson who was forty-one years and 257 days old when he played in the 1924 FA Cup final for Newcastle United.

Freddie Buck (centre-half), only 5ft 4ins tall, was one of the smallest centre-halves ever to appear in an FA Cup final. Born in Newcastle-under-Lyme, Staffs in July 1880, he played for Stafford Rangers before joining Albion in November 1900. However, he left The Hawthorns in May 1903 for Liverpool, switched to Plymouth Argyle in January 1904 before returning to Albion for a second spell in April 1906. Initially an inside forward, he switched to centre-half and went on to make 310 appearances for the Baggies, scoring ninety-four goals. A Second Division championship winner in 1911 and an FA Cup finalist in 1912, Fred represented the Football League and the Southern League. On leaving Albion he joined Swindon Town, served in the Army during World War One and later became a licensee in Stafford where he died in June 1952. A lot of Fred's memorabilia is on view in the WBA museum at The Hawthorns, loaned by members of his family.

Bobby McNeal (left-half) was a well-built, tough-tackling left-half who made 403 appearances for Albion (ten goals scored) between June 1910 and May 1925 (when he retired). Born in County Durham in January 1891, he played for Hobson Wanderers before moving to The Hawthorns. He helped Albion win the Second Division title in 1911, reach the FA Cup final in 1912 and win the First Division championship in 1920. Capped twice by England (v. Wales and Scotland) in 1914, he also represented the Football League on five occasions. He became a licensee after quitting football, and died in West Bromwich in May 1956.

Alan Claude Jephcott (outside-right) was a fast-raiding, direct outside-right, born in Smethwick on 30 October 1891, died at Penn, Wolverhampton on 5 October 1950. He played for Stourbridge and Brierley Hill Alliance before spending twelve years with WBA (April 1911 to May 1923). He won a League championship winner's medal in 1920 and scored sixteen goals in 190 appearances before a broken leg ended his career at the age of 31. A junior international, he also represented the Football league and an England XI and was unlucky not to win a full cap.

Harry Wright (inside-right) was a very useful inside-forward who scored twenty goals in 105 apps for WBA in two spells at the club: November 1906 to May 1909 and from June 1910 until November 1919 (helping Albion win the Second Division title in 1911 and playing in the FA Cup final of 1912). He played for Stourbridge in between his stints at The Hawthorns and in 1919-20 assisted Wolves. Later with Newport County, he retired in May 1922. Harry was born in West Bromwich on 12 October 1888 and died in the same town on 8 September 1950.

Bob Pailor (centre-forward) was a strong, hard-running centre-forward, born in Stockton-on-Tees in July 1887. He played for West Hartlepool before joining

Albion in October 1908. He remained at The Hawthorns for six years during which time he scored forty-seven goals in ninety-two appearances, gaining a Second Division championship medal in 1911 and an FA Cup runners-up medal in 1912. Transferred to Newcastle Utd in May 1914 for £1,550, Bob retired in May 1915 with a kidney complaint. He later became a bookmaker but sadly went blind. He died in Hartlepool.

Sid Bowser (inside-left) played as an inside-forward during the first eight years of his career and as a centre-half for the last ten. Born in Birmingham in April 1891, he had a trial with Birmingham before joining Albion as a forward in July 1908. After helping the Baggies win the Second Division title and reach the FA Cup in successive seasons, he surprised everyone by joining Distillery in Ireland in April 1913. Returning to The Hawthorns in February 1914 he then spent the next ten years as a defender, collecting a league championship winner's medal in 1920 when, in the home game against Bradford City, he scored a hat-trick of penalties from his centre-half position. He moved to Walsall in August 1924, after seventy-two goals in 371 games for Albion, and gaining an England cap (v. Ireland) in October 1919. Sid retired in May 1927 and became a publican in Dudley. He died in Birmingham in February 1961.

Ben Shearman (outside-left) was a line-hugging outside-left with fine shot. He played for WBA from June 1911 until July 1919 and scored eighteen goals in 143 first team appearances in those eight years. He played for Rotherham Town and Bristol City before joining Albion and after leaving played in turn for Nottingham Forest, Gainsborough Trinity and Norton Woodseats (as player-trainer-coach), retiring in May 1938. Born in Lincoln on 12 December 1884, Ben died on 21 October 1958 in Gainsborough.

Fans – in suits – travelling by horse-powered wagons, in London, to the 1912 Cup Final. **Bower Collection**

The Barnsley mascot 'Amos' outside the club's headquarters, the Clarence Hotel, Sheffield Road, one of Will Randall's 1912 photographic postcards. Bower Collection

19 FA Cup Final v West Bromwich Albion

Saturday 20 April 1912: Crystal Palace Grounds, Sydenham

Barnsley   0
WBA   0
Attendance   54,556

Match report taken from the *Barnsley Independent*:

How two well matched teams failed to score
GREAT DEFENCE

By 'Centre-Forward'

Although very disappointing in the respect that it was attended by no definite result the game between Barnsley and West Bromwich Albion was a better final tie than most of those which we have seen of recent years. The one thing needful to make it an interesting contest was some scoring. In the absence of even one goal the spectators who watched a strenuous winter game played in the genial warmth of summer were somewhat languid. They waited for thrills, and experienced none. I am convinced that the scoring of a goal by either side would

A rare 'Richard Coer De Lion' pen and ink drawing produced by H J Fletcher of Greenfoot Lane, Barnsley. Wearmouth Collection

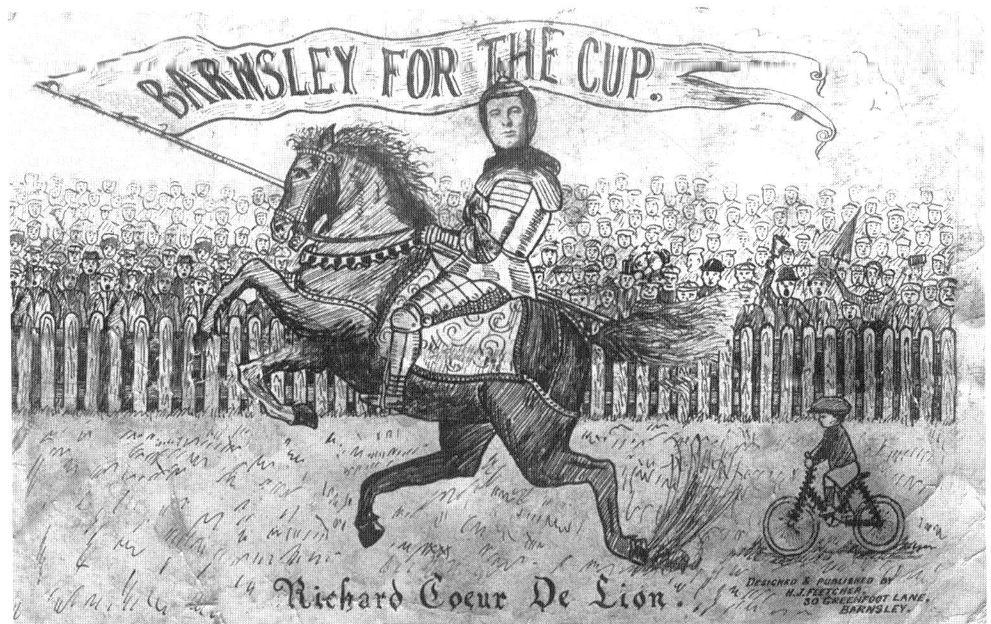

have awakened the onlookers to enthusiasm. It was a remarkably impartial crowd that gathered in somewhat smaller numbers than usual on the classic slopes of Sydenham. Barnsley followers, of course, were present and the Albion admirers with a shorter train journey to make were there in greater force but the bulk of the crowd was a metropolitan assemblage. Goals are the essence of football and the crowd would not have minded a drawn game if both sides had each scored twice or even three times. As it was they went away disappointed. Rarely if ever have I seen a football crowd at so important an event less excited. As for enthusiasm there was none.

Forwards Failure

Yet small was the fault of the players. Both teams tried hard enough to score, and the game was greater in pace and power, more prolific of swift exchanges then many English Cup Finals I have seen. As a matter of fact each side had a defence so skilful and resolute that it dominated the opposing attack. Moreover on the rare occasions when the backs were beaten the forwards of either side, possibly from over excitement failed to seize their chances, though each goal had more than one remarkably narrow escape. It was not a game wherein the goalkeepers were greatly troubled with; the advancing forwards were so often rendered powerless before they got to shooting range. When this was not the case their shots had little sting or accuracy about them, and neither custodian throughout the entire contest was called upon to stop a shot which he could have been pardoned for missing.

Albion's early attack

For the first twenty minutes or so the West Bromwich men were decidedly the smarter team, but their forwards, among whom Shearman was a conspicuous figure on the extreme left wing, failed to take advantage of an unsteady start by the Barnsley defence, who in the early stages were not in their true form, Downs being the shadow of his real self, and Taylor early on making a miss kick which might easily have let the Albion forwards through. Barnsley had their share of ill luck later in the game, but during this opening period they enjoyed some good luck, notably, when a furious drive by Pailor, which was going straight for the mark struck Downs in the chest, and again when in dealing with another fierce straight drive by Baddeley from half back, Cooper, who darted forward to take the ball allowed it to slip from his hands, happily however for the Yorkshireman the keeper was able to recover before an

Archie Taylor photographed at the 1912 Cup Final.
Wood Collection

The 1911-12 West Brom squad.
Wood Collection

Albion forward could reach him. Cooper's nerve, however, was not broken by this early interchange and a little later he was quite himself in smartly saving a dangerous header from Baddeley following a corner kick and then a pretty oblique shot from Jephcott.

Barnsley Brightening
Fortunate and successful opposition to the pressure of their foes made an occasional Barnsley attack flash past the Albion halves but they usually met their masters in Pennington and Cook. Then the Yorkshire attack improved and we saw some of the dash and speed that usually characterise the movements of the front rank. Bartrop was a conspicuous figure on the extreme right, and following the centre from him, Lillycrop from close quarters headed in, only to find Pearson quite safe as indeed the Albion custodian was throughout the struggle.

The packed Crystal Palace ground during the 1912 Cup Final. Notice how many rear spectators used stools to gain a vantage point. Wood Collection

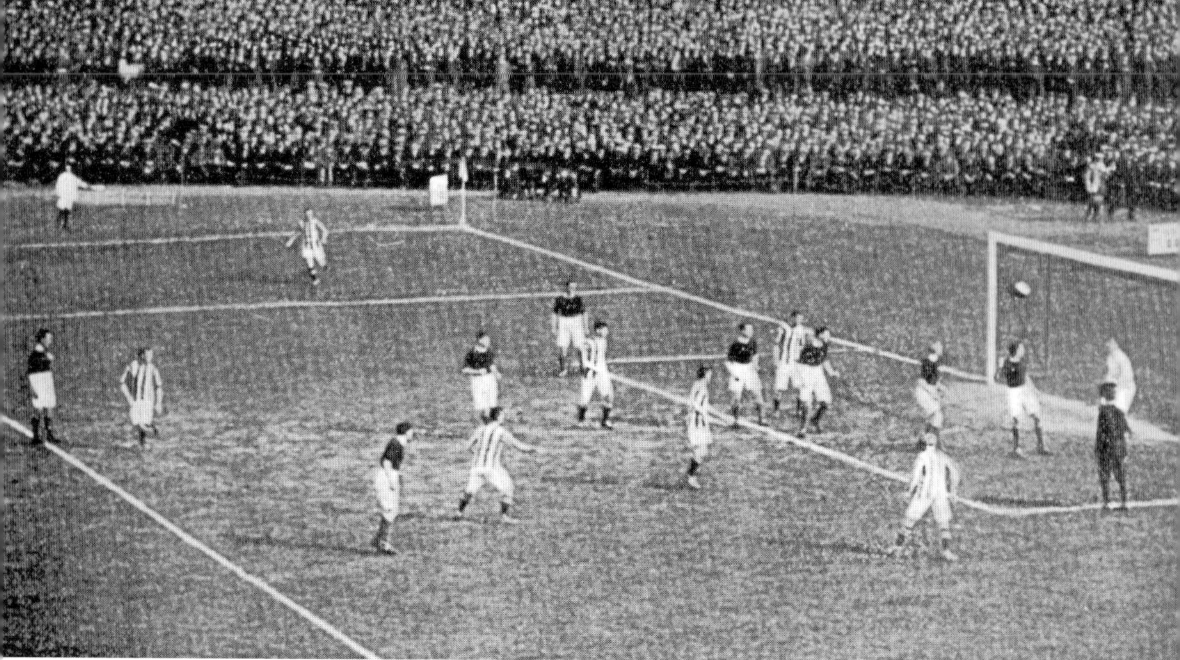

West Brom attack the Barnsley goal during the Crystal Palace FA Cup Final of 1912. Bower Collection

Nevertheless, the attacks of the Oakwell brigade were not equal to great defence of Pennington and Cook, who were admirable in their judgement and tackled skillfully and though Bartrop fired in a good long shot it was not good enough to beat Pearson. To Barnsley's increased dash the 'Throstles' responded gamely, and during the last few minutes of the first half, thanks in great measure to the sprightliness of their left winger, Shearman, they gave the Yorkshire defence a lively time. But Downs and Taylor had recovered from their early unsteadiness and, well assisted by the halves, gallantly held their own to the arrival of the interval.

Smart exchanges
After a change of ends we saw more of Barnsley as we had seen them against Bradford City at Bramall Lane. The vigour and speed of their forwards was wonderfully improved, and for the remainder of the match they were quite the equals of West Bromwich at all points. But the Albion continued to play smart football all round and the result was that we saw well-matched teams fighting for all they were worth in order to score, but fighting in vain. Swift and even were the exchanges, but Taylor at one end and Pennington at the other were like lions in the path of the eager forwards. Once, after a splendid sprint by Jephcott, the ball was sent to Shearman, who was given a good opening, only to shoot the ball against the side net. It was a really a fine chance of scoring which thus came to the Albion left-winger, but he was rather slow in working for a good position,

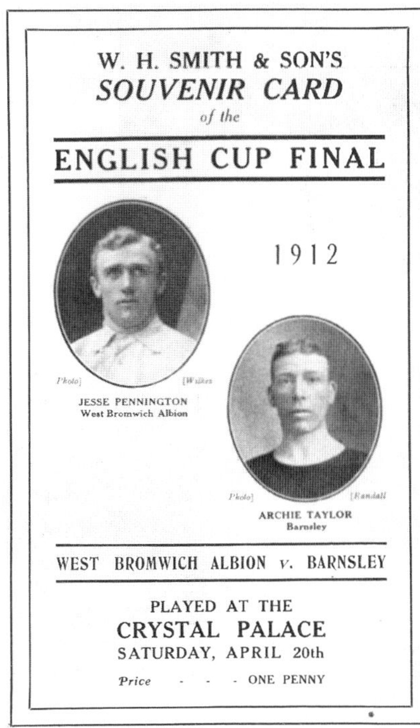

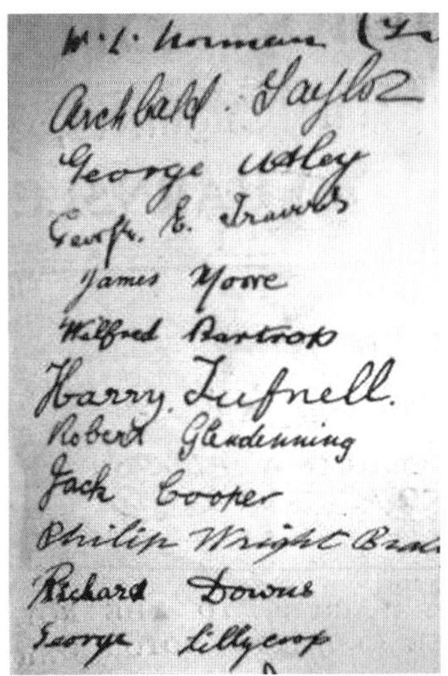

An autographed sheet containing the signatures of the FA Cup Final team.
Wood Collection

WH Smith's official and souvenir card of the 1912 Cup Final at Crystal Palace featured Jessie Pennington and Archie Taylor.
WH Smith

and by the time he shot Cooper had rushed across to reduce his room for shooting, and might possibly have saved even had the shot been on the mark.

An Exciting Episode

Barnsley were now more dangerous near goal than they had been, but still Pearson was equal to the work given him to do by Moore and Lillycrop. The Yorkshiremen following a centre by Moore made one desperate attack in the best dashing style and were certainly very unlucky not to score. In rapid succession four shots were driven in fiercely, to be intercepted in their flight, and it was certainly 'hard lines' for the Yorkshiremen to see one by Glendenning rebound from Pennington right in front and another by Tufnell strike the upright. This was the most exciting episode of the match, and the excitement rose as suddenly Shearman came sweeping away on the Albion left threatening danger to the Barnsley goal. He finished with a fine centre, but the inside men were not well up to seize it, and Cooper dashing out cleared before they came upon the scene. That one daring dash and fierce fusillade, wherein the Albion citadel escaped by sheer good fortune stands out as a prominent incident in the many fierce exchanges of a hotly contested second half.

Narrow escape

As the game went on the rivals continued to struggle gamely for a goal whereby to carry home the cup. Such was the character of the play that onlookers felt that one goal would be quite sufficient to settle the issue. Although tiring somewhat

A rare surviving ticket of the 1912 FA Cup Final.
Wood Collection

An equally rare dressing room pass.
Wood Collection

as the end drew near neither of the players ceased to strive and hope. Barnsley remembered their sensational finish at Bramall Lane and Albion that at Owlerton. In the last minutes each goal had more than one narrow escape, and each side had a corner, for the play continued to surge from end to end in a way that kept spectators hopeful that even yet one side or the other might score. Once Pearson kicked away a shot from Lillycrop and then right on time when Shearman sprinted away and centred Pailor came sailing in as he had done when he got the goal which beat the Rovers in the semi-final, but this time the Albion centre flashed the ball just outside instead of inside the post, and the Barnsley goal escaped. Then came the sound of the final whistle.

Barnsley won the toss to select the choice of ground for the replay and picked Bramall Lane.

Barnsley: Cooper, Taylor, Downs, Glendenning, Bratley, Utley, Bartrop, Tufnell, Lillycrop, Travers, Moore

WBA: Pearson, Cook, Pennington, Baddeley, Buck, McNeal, Jephcott, Wright, Pailor, Bowser, Shearman

20 FA Cup Final Replay v West Bromwich Albion

Wednesday 24 April 1912: Bramall Lane, Sheffield

Barnsley   1   (Tufnell)
WBA   0
Attendance: 38,555

Match report from the *Barnsley Independent*:

THE FINAL AT THE LANE

Many missed chances in moderate game

TUFNELL'S GOAL

By 'Centre-Forward'

The fight is over. Barnsley have won the English Cup. So well matched were the heroes of Oakwell and the Albion of West Bromwich, both at the Crystal Palace on Saturday and again at Bramall Lane yesterday that not until they had struggled strenuously against each other for 90 minutes at Sydenham and 118 minutes at Sheffield was either team able to score a goal. Then, when we were all becoming resigned to a third meeting at Everton, next Tuesday, suddenly came the one thing being desired – a goal. Tufnell, Barnsley's inside-right, was the hero. Getting the ball in midfield, he made for the Albion citadel with promptitude and alacrity by the nearest route. Distancing Pennington and Cook, the Albion backs, who made a vain effort to check his career, Tufnell kept complete control of the ball, and when Pearson advanced to lessen his space for shooting, he directed it deftly, skilfully, and accurately into the far corner of the net. By that goal, scored two minutes from time, Barnsley won the cup and great was the rejoicing thereafter.

A Great Achievement
Apart from the fact that they scored a goal, the winners played no better than did the losers. But that goal was a very fine one, and goals are what football teams play for. Therefore did Barnsley deserve their victory. For their triumph they have had to work very hard, taking part in no fewer than twelve games in their progress through the six rounds and last evening they received the most coveted of all football trophies from the hands of Mr JC Clegg. By dour defence, indomitable pluck, dashing attack, and a fair share of that good luck without

Bramall Lane, Sheffield, soon to be the scene for a memorable FA Cup Final replay. Wood Collection

which the English Cup was never yet won the Barnsley team have kept the Cup, which Bradford City won a year ago, in Yorkshire. For a Second Division league club to remove from their path such powerful foes as Barnsley have done, and won the blue ribbon of football is indeed a great achievement. The heroic Oakwell brigade deserve all the congratulations and commendations that will be showered upon them.

Coincidence

Although Sheffield football enthusiasts suffered for the usual early eclipse of their own clubs, Wednesday and United, they have seen plenty of good sport this season provided by other clubs. And what a remarkable coincidence it has been that in the three great games played in the cutlery city the issue should have been left for the closing movements of the game to decide, and in each case in extra time. It was with absolutely the last kick of the match that Lillycrop beat and dismissed Bradford City from the fourth round at Bramall lane. Two minutes from time Pailor, the West Bromwich centre forward scored the goal which removed Blackburn Rovers from the semi-final at Owlerton, and the same brief space remained for play when Tufnell yesterday made that brilliant individual effort which sent the clever West Bromwich lads home beaten, and gave the cup to Barnsley. No goalless draws have been seen in Sheffield, but three dramatic finishes to well-contested games.

Narrow escapes

Brilliant weather, a brisk breeze blowing from goal to goal, and a fast, hard ground on which the lively ball was not easy to keep under complete control, were the conditions under which the battle commenced. That the 'Throstles' should have done the more pressing with the wind behind them is not surprising. But they also played the smarter and more scientific football, faulty shooting and inability to seize chances being however a serious fault. Barnsley, though making fewer attacks, the attacks were usually dangerous. It was a Barnsley man, Moore to wit, who sent in the only real good shot before half time, and this was admirably saved by Pearson, who is a cool and skilful custodian. Twice, however, before the change of ends would the Albion's able custodian have been

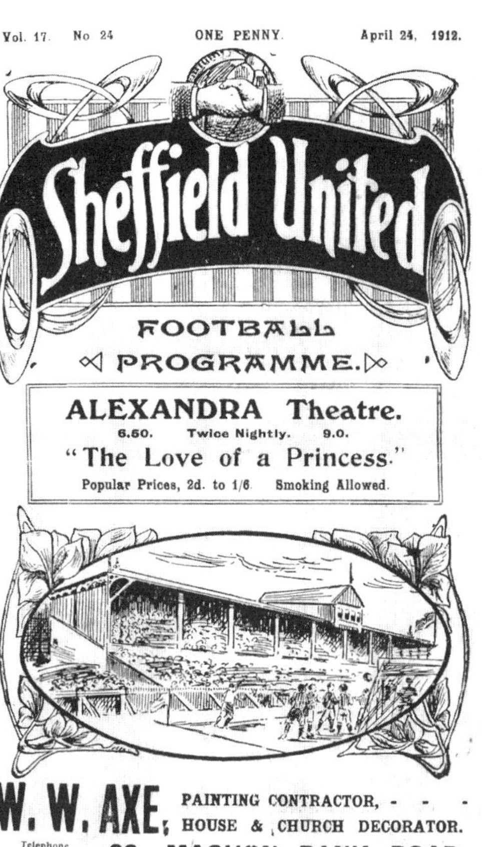

Match programme for the 1912 FA Cup Final replay at Bramall Lane. Wood Collection

beaten but for the happy inspiration first of Baddeley and then of Cook, to be almost under the bar just in the right place to hook the ball away.

Well matched teams

After much even play in the second half, some of it rather tame, there was an equally exciting scene and an equally narrow escape of the Barnsley citadel when Cooper stopped a stinging shot from Pailor without being able to clear, and Glendenning swept into the goalmouth to save a desperate situation. There was little to choose between the teams during this half. The Albion attacks had more sting now against the wind than there had been with it, and near the end of the ninety minutes Cooper twice distinguished himself in first stopping a low fast drive where with young Jephcott finished a sparkling sprint and a moment afterwards tipping over the bar a superbly high shot from Bowser. The crowd were eager for goals, but none came to please them, and when time arrived the palpable explanation of the state of the game was clear superiority of the defence over the attack.

This somewhat blurred but historic still-frame image shows the moment when Harry Tufnell scored Barnsley's winning goal at Bramall Lane. Wood Collection

Final Efforts
In the early parts of the extra half hour West Bromwich played brighter smart football, and Shearman with a wonderful centre gave the other forwards a glorious opening but three men missed it. Another centre by their left-winger was utilised by Pailor to shoot splendidly, but a brilliant save by Cooper amid seething excitement saved the situation. The Albion earnestly claimed a penalty for Wright being fetched down but the referee was prompt in his refusal. The last quarter of an hour was Barnsley's. West Bromwich were fortunate when with Pearson out of his goal two quickly succeeding shots rebounded from other defenders who swamped in front of the unprotected net. Still the Midlanders were not done with, and Cooper had again to bestir himself to save a header by Pailor. Both sides fought on gallantly with the pace and vigour of their efforts telling upon them, and when Tufnell darted ahead and scored the one goal of the match Cook and Pennington had neither of them the speed to overtake him. So Barnsley won, and South Yorkshire is the proudest part of England today.

About the players
Both Cooper and Pearson are exceptionally good goalkeepers. Cooper had the more difficult shots to deal with yesterday.

The whole defence of Barnsley was very fine, Downs and Taylor both playing in great style, while there was not a weak spot in the half-back line where no man played better than Bratley. Though Cook and Pennington both played a good sound game for the Albion at the back, the famous English international was not in the great form he showed on Saturday at the Palace. The middle line of the Midlanders were clever and strong to a man. Forward, the Albion were the more skilful combination, being artful and accurate in their advances, Jephcott and Shearman, the extreme wingers perhaps being the most prominent. On the chances they had the 'Throstles' ought to have won but they finished weak. Barnsley's sudden dangerous dashes were the cause of much anxiety to the opposing defence. Early in the game Bartrop was a prominent figure. Lillycrop made good passes out to the wings, but was not particularly dangerous near goal. Tufnell, with his glorious goal was, of course, the hero of the day.

Barnsley: Cooper, Taylor, Downs, Glendenning, Bratley, Utley, Bartrop, Tufnell, Lillycrop, Travers, Moore

West Bromwich Albion: Cook, Pennington, Baddeley, Buck, McNeal, Jephcott, Wright, Pailor, Bowser, Shearman

Presentation Ceremony
A great crowd surged round the directors' box in the stand almost where the English cup stood shining on its plinth for all to see. Taylor led his worthy warspent men into the box. Mr J.C. Clegg, presenting the Cup said: 'I am quite sure that we are all exceedingly thankful that the strenuous games that we have seen are at last ended, and I am certain that you will agree with me in congratulating both winners and losers on going through some most strenuous and trying matches. We have been looking anxiously, but not half as anxiously as the players for a goal. I am thankful to say that it came at last [laughter] – and I am certain the players are more so, even those who have not succeeded today.'

True Sportsmen
'But both sides have shown what true sportsmen can do, and our congratulations may be given to those who have lost equally as to those who have won, and so long as the spirit that has been shown today is always shown on the football field I venture to predict that the game will still remain as it is now, the most popular game of sport [Cheers]. It would be invidious to mention names yet I feel that there is one to whom I must refer – I mean Pennington. [Enthusiastic cheers] he is a representative man of what is best in sport and one of our most prominent players and he has shown today and on every other occasion how the game should be played. His example has been followed by all the players of both sides.'

Players' Speeches
Taylor, perspiring, got a great ovation. In reply he said: 'I am sure you will agree with me that Barnsley deserve what they have got today. We have played very hard, so have West Bromwich. I thank you on behalf of this gift [laughter] - which we have won on behalf of the town of Barnsley.'

West Bromwich captain Pennington said: 'I congratulate Barnsley on their victory. I am very disappointed, as I know they are waiting for the cup at West Bromwich. There is one thing I should like to compliment Barnsley upon, as did Mr Clegg - that is the spirit they have shown in the match, which is a great example to footballers, and also to the spectators who followed it.' [Loud cheers] Sir Joseph Walton, MP for Barnsley, who was on Mr Clegg's right-hand, was bubbling over with pride and enthusiasm at the accomplishment of the men of Barnsley. In composing a vote of thanks to Mr JC Clegg for his attendance, he said after many years representation of

George Utley's cup-winners medal in its original case.
Linzi Henry

The cup-winner's medal of George Travers (reverse side). Wood Collection

Barnsley he was prouder of the town today than he had ever been in his life.

Sir Joseph's praise

'Barnsley have stuck to it and at last they have achieved the greatest victory in the football field and we take home to Barnsley a magnificent trophy. At the same time we can join in saying though Barnsley have deserved it they had in West Bromwich Albion foemen worthy of their steel. They have shown that they are made of British pluck, self-reliance and skill that are the greatest sporting instincts of old England. We sympathise with West Bromwich in their defeat, and only hope that they, like Barnsley, will stick to their task and once again take home the Cup.' [Cheers] Viscount Lewisham, MP for West Bromwich, seconded the vote and confessed that he shared Pennington's disappointment, but he hoped he was sufficient of a sportsman to be able on behalf of West Bromwich to offer sincere congratulations to Barnsley on their victory. He was a bit of a Yorkshireman himself, and if it was not West Bromwich to win he would as soon see a Yorkshire team win as any. He hoped that the same teams would meet in the final next year - and that the result would be reversed. [Laughter and cheers]

HOW BARNSLEY WELCOMED THE ENGLISH CUP

A tremendous reception awaited the homecoming of the Cup winners last night. The news of the match was awaited with feverish interest, and when the result became known there were scenes of the wildest enthusiasm in the main streets. The team, with the officials, as arranged, motored home, and long before their arrival about nine o'clock the Sheffield road and main thoroughfare was almost packed solid with the enthusiastic thousands. In fact it seemed as though every living soul in the town had come outside to receive the heroes.

At the Boundary

The Territorial Band awaited the arrival of the successful motor party at the borough boundary and played lively airs, heading the procession playing 'See the conquering hero comes' which with difficulty made their way along

The FA Cup on display at Oakwell in 1912. Bower Collection

The chaotic but good natured scene on Queen Street, Barnsley, as the crowd awaits the result from the Crystal Palace of the FA Cup Final. *Bower Collection*

The triumphant Barnsley players with the FA Cup, in a charabanc outside the club headquarters, the Clarence Hotel. *Wood Collection*

Sheffield Road. A tour of the town had been arranged, but the crowd around the Clarence hotel, the club's headquarters, was so dense that a halt had to be called. The players were received with a storm of applause, and the Cup proudly held aloft was the cause for prolonged demonstration.

The victorious Barnsley FC players and directors in 1912
Bower Collection

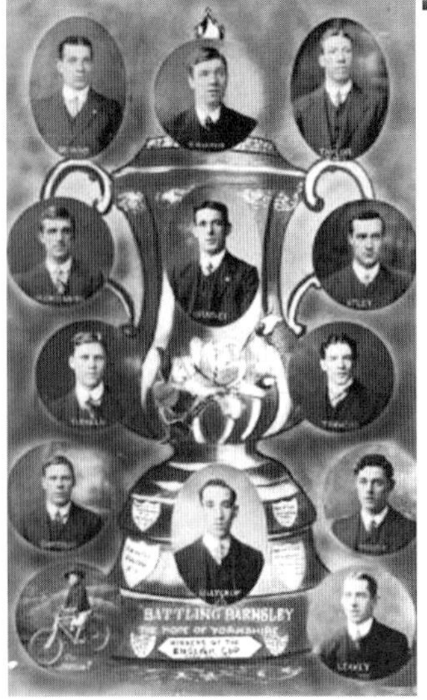

The winners, with Little Sammy, the Barnsley mini-mascot. Bower Collection

Cheering Thousands

The players and officials entered the hotel, and from the balcony the Mayor [Councillor J H Cotterill], Alderman J S Rose JP [chairman of the club] and several players made congratulatory speeches. The intense enthusiasm prevailed during the night, and probably the town has never before seen such enthusiasm.

The Gate

The attendance was not a record for Bramall Lane. The number of people paying for admission, including those who had purchased tickets at the office was 38,555. The receipts amounted to £2,615 9s (worth about £149,238 today).

The collection in aid of the Titanic Fund amounted to £49 1s 6d of which amount £37 was in coppers. The boxes were taken round by the Sheffield United players, assisted by some of the Wednesday players.

George Travers's cup-winners medal. Wood Collection

Another imaginative postcard by Will Randall showing portraits of the 1912 cup winners. We owe much to Randall for his portrait images of the Barnsley players. Bower Collection

This imaginative Will Randall postcard uses Barnsley's fame as a coal town in commemorating the great 1912 FA Cup win. Wood Collection

1911/1912

6th in Division Two
P38 W15 D12 L11 F45 A42

#	Date	Opponents	Res	Att	Goalscorers	Clegg JA	Downs JT	Taylor A	Glendenning R	Boyle TW	Utley G	Bartrop W	Travers JE	Lillycrop GB	Tufnell H	Leavey HJ	Cornock M	Hanlon E	Moore J	Mitchell R	Wilcock GH	Martin F	Bratley PW	Cooper JC	Roystone A	Hall JE	Doncaster T	Barson F	Jebb A	Wigmore C
1	2-Sep A	Huddersfield Town	1 - 2	12,000	Tufnell	1	2	3	4	5	6	7	8	9	10	11														
2	9-Sep H	Blackpool	1 - 0	7,000	Boyle	1	2	3	4	5	6	7	8	9	10	11														
3	11-Sep A	Birmingham	3 - 1	5,000	Cornock 2, Tufnell	1	2	3	4	5	6	7		8	10	11	9													
4	16-Sep A	Glossop	2 - 0	2,000	Cornock, Tufnell	1	2	3	4	5	6	7		8	10	11	9													
5	23-Sep H	Hull City	1 - 2	9,000	Lillycrop	1	2	3	4	5	6	7		8	10	11	9													
6	26-Sep A	Grimsby Town	0 - 0	5,000		1	2	3	4		6	7		8	10	11	9	5												
7	30-Sep H	Burnley	1 - 1	7,000	Cornock	1	2	3	4		6	7		8	10	11	9	5												
8	7-Oct A	Bradford Park Avenue	0 - 1	20,000		1	2	3	4		6			9	10	11		5	7	8										
9	14-Oct H	Fulham	2 - 2	7,000	Tufnell, Cornock	1	2	3	4		6			8	10	11	9	5	7											
10	21-Oct A	Derby County	0 - 0	8,000			2	3	4		6			8	10	11	9	5	7		1									
11	28-Oct H	Stockport County	2 - 1	6,000	Lillycrop 2		2	3	4		6			8	10	11	9	5	7		1									
12	4-Nov A	Leeds City	2 - 3	10,000	Hanlon, Leavey		2	3	4		6	7		8	10	11		5			1	9								
13	11-Nov H	Wolverhampton Wanderers	2 - 1	8,000	Martin, Utley		2	3	4		6	7		8	10	11					1	9	5							
14	18-Nov A	Leicester Fosse	0 - 0	6,000			2	3	4		6	7		8	10	11						9	5	1						
15	25-Nov H	Gainsborough Trinity	4 - 0	5,000	Geenton og, Bartrop 2, Utley		2	3	4		6	7		8	10							9	5	1	11					
16	9-Dec H	Nottingham Forest	1 - 0	5,000	Tufnell		2	3	4		6	7		8	10	11						9	5	1						
17	16-Dec A	Chelsea	1 - 2	25,000	Lillycrop		2	3	4		6	7		8	10	11						9	5	1						
18	23-Dec H	Clapton Orient	2 - 1	6,000	Lillycrop, Utley		2	3			6	7	8	9	10	11							5	1		4				
19	25-Dec H	Bristol City	4 - 1	12,000	Lillycrop, Utley, Travers, Tufnell		2	3			6	7	8	9	10	11							5	1		4				
20	26-Dec A	Bristol City	1 - 0	6,000	Tufnell		2	3			6	7	8	9	10	11							5	1		4				
21	1-Jan H	Huddersfield Town	0 - 0	12,000			2	3			6	7	8	9	10	11							5	1		4				
22	6-Jan A	Blackpool	0 - 0	2,000			2	3	4		6	7	8	9	10	11							5	1						
23	27-Jan A	Hull City	0 - 0	10,000			2	3	4		6	7	8	9	10	11							5	1						
24	10-Feb H	Bradford Park Avenue	1 - 0	5,000	Travers			3	4		6	7	8	9	10	11							5	1		2				
25	12-Feb A	Burnley	0 - 3				2	3	4		6		8	9	10	11		5	7					1						
26	17-Feb A	Fulham	2 - 2	20,000	Leavey, Tufnell		2	3	4		6		8	9	10	11			7				5	1						
27	2-Mar A	Stockport County	1 - 1	7,000	Tufnell		2	3	4		6	7	8		10	11	9	5						1						
28	16-Mar A	Wolverhampton Wanderers	0 - 5	6,000			2		4		6	7	8	9		11	10	5						1		3				
29	23-Mar H	Leicester Fosse	0 - 0	4,000			2					7	8	9				5	11					1	10		3	4	6	
30	6-Apr H	Grimsby Town	2 - 2	5,000	Bartrop, Lillycrop		2	3	4		6	7	8	9	10				11				5	1						
31	8-Apr H	Birmingham	1 - 0	5,000	Lillycrop		2	3	4		6	7	8	9	10				11				5	1						
32	10-Apr A	Gainsborough Trinity	2 - 1		Lloyd og, Moore		2		4			7	8				10	5	11	9				1			3		6	
33	11-Apr H	Leeds City	3 - 4		Tufnell, Travers 2		2	3	5			7	8		10				11			9		1				4	6	
34	13-Apr A	Nottingham Forest	2 - 0	7,000	Lillycrop, Tufnell		2	3	4		6	7		9	8				11				5	1						10
35	22-Apr H	Derby County	0 - 2	5,000			2	3	4		6	7	8	9	10				11				5	1						
36	25-Apr H	Chelsea	0 - 2	7,000			2		4		6	7	8	9	10				11				5	1			3			
37	27-Apr A	Clapton Orient	0 - 2				2	3				7	8				9	5	11	10				1			4	6	
38	29-Apr H	Glossop	1 - 0	2,000	Glendenning		2		4		6	7	8		10				11				5	1			3			9
		League Apps				9	37	33	32	5	34	32	22	33	34	27	12	13	16	3	4	7	19	25	2	6	4	3	4	2
		Goals							1	1	4	3	4	9	11	2	5	1	1			1								

FA Cup

Rd	Date	Opponents	Res	Att	Goalscorers	Clegg JA	Downs JT	Taylor A	Glendenning R	Boyle TW	Utley G	Bartrop W	Travers JE	Lillycrop GB	Tufnell H	Leavey HJ	Cornock M	Hanlon E	Moore J	Mitchell R	Wilcock GH	Martin F	Bratley PW	Cooper JC	Roystone A	Hall JE	Doncaster T	Barson F	Jebb A	Wigmore C
R1	13-Jan A	Birmingham	0 - 0	18,000	£489		2	3	4		6	7	10	9	8	11							5	1						
R1r	22-Jan H	Birmingham	3 - 0	12,000	Lillycrop 25,66, Tufnell 51 (£395)		2	3	4		6	7	10	9	8	11							5	1						
R2	3-Feb H	Leicester Fosse	1 - 0	15,114	Lillycrop 60 (£493)		2	3	4		6	7	10	9	8	11							5	1						
R3	24-Feb A	Bolton Wanderers	2 - 1	34,598	Lillycrop 46, Leavey 53 £1175		2	3	4		6	7	10	9	8	11							5	1						
R4	9-Mar H	Bradford City	0 - 0	24,987	£1,488		2	3	4		6	7	10	9	8	11							5	1						
R4r	13-Mar A	Bradford City	0 E 0	31,910	£1,260		2	3	4		6	7	10	9	8	11							5	1						
R4rr	18-Mar N	Bradford City	0 A 0	37,000	(Elland Road) £1322		2	3	4		6	7	10	9	8	11							5	1						
R4rrr	21-Mar N	Bradford City	3 E 2	38,264	Lillycrop 84, 119 Travers 16 (Bramall Lane) £1490		2	3	4		6	7	10	9	8				11				5	1						
SF	30-Mar N	Swindon Town	0 - 0	48,057	(Stamford Bridge) £2985		2	3	4		6	7	10	9	8				11				5	1						
SFr	3-Apr N	Swindon Town	1 - 0	18,000	Bratley (Meadow Lane) £1038		2	3	4		6	7	10	9	8				11				5	1						
Fin	20-Apr N	West Bromwich Albion	0 - 0	54,556	(Crystal Palace)		2	3	4		6	7	10	9	8				11				5	1						
Finr	24-Apr N	West Bromwich Albion	1 E 0	38,555	Tufnell (Bramall Lane) £2600		2	3	4		6	7	10	9	8				11				5	1						
		FA Cup Apps				0	12	12	12	0	12	12	12	12	12	7	0	0	5	0	0	0	12	12	0	0	0	0	0	0

PART SIX

Champions of the World

'Championship of the World' game at Celtic Park, Glasgow
Tuesday 3 September 1912

Glasgow Celtic	1	(Loney, 55 minutes)
Barnsley	1	(Moore, 40 minutes)

Victory in the FA Cup final saw Barnsley invited to play the Scottish Cup winners Celtic at Celtic Park at the commencement of the following season. The match was the third in a series grandiosely billed as the 'Championship of the World'. Following defeats for English Cup winners West Bromwich Albion against Renton in 1888 and League Champions Aston Villa against Scottish Champions Celtic in 1910 the Yorkshire side became the first English side to avoid defeat by drawing 1-1. In fact, with a little bit of luck, Barnsley might have returned victorious as for much of what proved to be an entertaining game they were the better side. Barnsley fielded the eleven that had enjoyed success against WBA at the 1912 FA Cup final. Celtic had won the Scottish Cup by defeating Clyde at Ibrox on 6 April 1912 with goals from Gallagher and McMenemy.

The sides were as follows:

Celtic: Mulrooney, McGregor, Dodds, Young, Loney, Mitabell, McAtee, Gallagher, Johnstone, McMenemy Gray

Barnsley: Cooper, Downs, Taylor, Glendenning, Bratley, Utley, Bartrop, Tufnell, Lillycrop, Travers, Moore

The match itself was poorly attended, heavy rain reducing the crowd from the expected 20 to 30 thousand to just 4,000 and they could easily have seen the visitors take a first minute lead except for a fine John Mulrooney save from Moore. The Celtic keeper then had to be down smartly to block hard drives from Glendenning and Bartrop as Barnsley's quick passing game opened up the Glasgow side's defence. When the home side did push forward they found Cooper in commanding form and although much of the game became bogged down in midfield it was no surprise when with five minutes of the first half remaining that Barnsley took a deserved lead. The goal came when Travers and Moore linked up on the left before the latter let fly a shot that the Celtic keeper could hardly have seen never mind stopped. At half time the scoreline thus stood at Celtic 0 Barnsley 1.

The second half was a much more even affair especially after the Scottish side equalised in the 55th minute, Willie Loney scoring from the penalty spot after the referee spotted a handball in the penalty area. The game then flowed from box to box but try as both sets of forwards might they were unable to create sufficient chances to finish off their opponents and at the end of the 90 minutes both teams were probably content to have finished up equal with Barnsley having shown an initially sceptical Scottish crowd and press box that their FA Cup victory had been no fluke.

Barnsley FC's Cup Heroes: Pen Portraits

1 FAIRCLOUGH, Arthur (Manager)
1896-1919; 1928-30; 1935   466 Games

Born: 23 March 1874, Redbrook, Barnsley
1896-97 BARNSLEY director, 1898-May1901; BARNSLEY Secretary, 1904-12; BARNSLEY manager, c1912-Dec1919; Huddersfield Town manager, Feb1920-May1927; Leeds United manager, May1928-May1930; Barnsley manager 1935 BARNSLEY director

Arthur's playing career was very short-lived as a serious injury in his teens forced him to retire from the game in 1891. He embarked on a successful spell of refereeing and participated in the Midland League and FA Cup competitions before moving to Oakwell as a director in 1896. Barnsley had just joined the Midland League and after a couple of successful seasons they were elected to the Football League at the first attempt. To meet the increased organisational demands the club appointed Arthur to the role of secretary and he was to be responsible for the day to day running of the club and the signing of players, but not team selection as this was still to be done by a committee of directors. The early days were very hand to mouth with money difficult to come by. He organised the club into becoming a limited company in July 1900 and also oversaw major ground improvements which were required to keep the club in the League. Unfortunately progress on the field remained slow and coupled with business commitments he offered his

Arthur Fairclough.
Bower Collection

resignation at the end of the 1900-01 season. In parting, he recommended Barnsley's experienced full-back John McCartney as his replacement and the board took his advice and promoted the Scot to secretary/manager. McCartney had three successful years and when he accepted a position with St Mirren, Arthur was induced to return to the helm. The early part of his second spell saw a knack for uncovering talent with the likes of Jackie Mordue and George Reeves arriving from non league football. Together they transformed the fortunes of the team and the profits generated by their sales brought financial security to the club, but the moves proved very unpopular with the fans and the backlash was felt in a fall in attendances. From this stable base Arthur rebuilt the side with a mixture of journeymen, raw talent and local youths notably Boyle, Utley and Glendenning who would all later go on to captain First Division sides. They played a hard, uncompromising brand of football that drew comments from quarters that they were a dirty team. The truth was they were physical unit that could play football but they possessed a level of fitness that would enable them to grind out results. This ability to fight and wear down opponents was noted by the press who christened the club 'Battling Barnsley'. After the success of 1912 he accepted a large financial offer to manage Huddersfield Town and steered the fledgling league club through a very difficult period, being joined by Bill Norman in 1913. After the War, with Town heavily in debt and on the verge of extinction, he supported a proposed move to Elland Road to replace the expelled Leeds City. He also didn't endear himself to the Huddersfield public when they found out that he had arranged to act as receiver should the club fold. The scandal made his position untenable and his offer to resign in December 1919 was accepted. Two months later the Town chairman who had also proposed the move took over at the newly-formed Leeds United and appointed Arthur its first manager. In 1923 he was again united with Bill Norman who became his assistant manager and together they took Leeds into the First Division at the first attempt. In 1928, at the age of fifty-five, he took control of Barnsley for a third time but resigned two years later and returned to the club once again in 1935 as a director.

	League		FA Cup	
	Gm	Pos	Gm	Rnd
1898-1899	34	11	6	Q5r
1899-1900	34	16	2	Q4
1900-1901	34	15	3	Q5

1904-1905	34	7	3	Int
1905-1906	38	12	4	2
1906-1907	38	8	5	4
1907-1908	38	16	1	1
1908-1909	38	17	1	1
1909-1910	38	9	9	RU
1910-1911	38	19	2	2
1911-1912	38	6	12	W
1928-1929	42	16	1	3
1929-1930	42	17	1	3
Totals	416		50	

2. NORMAN, William Lewis (Trainer)
1903-1905;1906-13

Born: circa 1873, Gazeley, Suffolk
1903-05 BARNSLEY trainer; 1905 Small Heath trainer; 1906-13
BARNSLEY trainer; 1913 Huddersfield Town trainer; 1919-23
Blackpool manager; Jun1923-27 Leeds United assistant
manager; Aug1927-Apr1932 Hartlepools United manager

Bill was a retired Army sergeant and joined the
club in 1903. He brought with him his experience
of military fitness drills and discipline and must
take some of the credit for the success of the side
by providing its battling stamina. Always a tough
trainer, he broke his service with a season at
Birmingham in 1905 but returned to Oakwell
straight after and remained until 1913. Bill's
sessions were noted for starting at 10am prompt
and, as was the norm in those days, training did
not involve any ball work. His method to achieve
player fitness involved stamina-building exercises
and sixty circuits of the field were the daily
morning routine. Running or walking it didn't
matter so long as the men kept moving and he was
even known to bring the players back in the
afternoon to do more of the same. After the success

Bill Norman.
Bower Collection

of 1912 he announced he was leaving for Huddersfield Town along with Arthur Fairclough but changed his mind to stay on before eventually making the move twelve months later. After the War he became Blackpool's first ever team manager and in four seasons with the Seasiders they pushed for promotion three times. Following an amount of criticism, he moved on to become Fairclough's assistant at Leeds United in 1923 and together they won promotion to the top division at the first attempt. After relegation in 1927 he resigned to take up the reins at Hartlepools where he stayed for five seasons, leaving just before his death in 1932. He was always respected by the players who affectionately called him 'The Sergeant Major' and often kept in touch with his past charges with one such incident almost ending in tragedy. Prior to the 1904 season he was up in Scotland preparing former Barnsley full-back Alf West for a sprint handicap when a serious accident occurred. The Liverpool player was crouched down set for his last 75-yard run of the day but his trainer was not ready and asked him to get up. As the athlete walked out of sight, Bill moved the barrel of the starting revolver round to the loaded chamber and was surprised when it fired. It was only on raising his head that he saw Alf had moved directly in front of the muzzle fully taking the shot. Fortunately Alf was not seriously hurt and in time made a full recovery, even scoring the goal that knocked Barnsley out of the FA Cup in 1906.

3. BARTROP, Charles Henry Wilfred
1909-14   178 appearances and 17 Goals
Born: 22 November 1887, Worksop
Ht 5'8" Wt 11-12
Outside Right
Worksop Town; BARNSLEY, June 1909-14; Liverpool 1914 (3 appearances).
Barnsley debut: aged 21 years 287 days, away to Glossop North End, 4 September 1909 (lost 3-0)

Played 1910 and 1912 Finals
Described as being 'a pacey outside right with the build of a ploughman', Wilf signed for the club on 21 June 1909 after coming to the attention of Arthur Fairclough. He noticed the youngster playing in the same division as Barnsley Reserves and joined from his local team Worksop Town after representing the League in the annual 'Champions v the Rest' match. He quickly made the step up from Midland League football, making his debut at Glossop in the second game of the season, replacing Ernest Coulthard on the right-wing. Throughout the Cup runs Wilf remained an ever present on the right-wing and in 1910 he scored the opener against Bristol Rovers and a wonder goal from the touchline in a 1-0 quarter-final win over Queen's Park Rangers. At the end of the 1913-

Wilf Bartrop.
Wood Collection

14 season he was transferred to Liverpool along with team-mate Phil Bratley where the local press announced 'Barnsley Brilliants bought for Anfield' but the outbreak of the First World War put their debuts in doubt. Against a sizeable public opinion the Football League decided to continue with organised football to boost morale but Wilf was in direct competition with the infamous Jackie Sheldon for the right-wing berth and made just three appearances before the season's end. A few weeks after the end of the campaign it emerged that Sheldon was the ring leader in a match fixing scandal and several other players were implicated. The following season would have seen Wilf naturally take the disgraced Sheldon's place in the side but the League decided to suspend the competition for the duration of the war. Wilf joined the Royal Field Artillery as a Gunner in a Trench Mortar Battery and and was unfortunately killed in Belgium, on 7 November 1918, just four days from the end of the war. In 2008, his 1912 FA Cup winners medal was sold for £14,400 – more than twice its estimate price, and in the December of that year a descendant (Peter Holland) published a biography of Wilf's life and times ontitled *Swifter than the Arrow.*

| | League | | FA Cup | |
	App	Gls	App	Gls
1909-1910	33	2	9	2
1910-1911	26	3	2	
1911-1912	32	3	12	
1912-1913	31	3	1	
1913-1914	30	4	2	
Totals	152	15	26	2

4. BOYLE, Thomas (Tommy) William
1906-11   174 appearances and 19 goals

Born: 29 January 1886, Hoyland
Ht 5'7" Wt 12-0
Centre-half/Right-half
Hoyland Star, Elsecar Athletic; September 1906 BARNSLEY; September 1911 to Burnley (210 appearances, 36 goals); 1923 to Wrexham (7 appearances)
Barnsley debut: aged 20 years 299 days, away to Chelsea, 24 November 1906 (lost 2-1)

Played 1910 Final

Despite his diminutive stature, Tommy was a commanding player in the air with fine distribution skills and an astute tactical brain. He was signed from local football in September 1906 after Arthur Fairclough spotted the youngster playing for Elsecar against Rockingham Colliery. Within two months he was making his debut at Chelsea, replacing William Ruddlesdin at right-half and the London press were certainly impressed with his performance. From that moment he remained an ever present in the half-back line along side Billy Silto and Arnold Oxspring. Tommy cemented his place in the side in the intervening years; and when Silto was transferred to Swindon

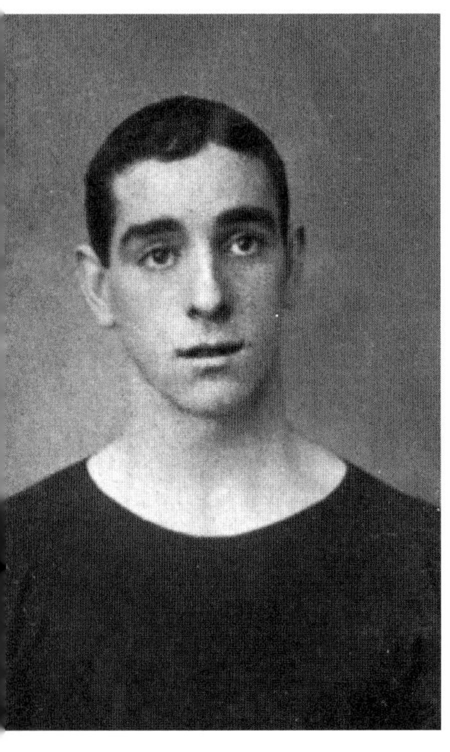

Tommy Boyle.
Bower Collection

1909, Tommy took over his centre-half berth and the captaincy of the club. The switch saw a dramatic effect on his goal scoring as he also assumed the penalty taking role and towards the end of the season bagged six goals in a thirteen-game spell, half of them from the spot. He was an ever present in the 1910 Cup side where he captained the team to within five minutes of victory only to lose his chance of a winner's medal in the replay. Following the disastrous season of 1910/11, when Barnsley had to apply for re-election, he was sold for a record fee of £1,250 to Burnley in September 1911. The move caused uproar throughout the town, the club and its supporters. The players publically released a statement to the fact that they were 'saddened to lose such a great player', strong critical letters appeared in the press, supporters returned season tickets to the club and his manager went as far as to describe him as 'a gem among jewels'. In 1913, he made his England debut in the Ireland game alongside former team mate George Utley and the subsequent year saw him finally gain his FA Cup winner's medal as the Clarets triumphed over Liverpool. After the war he went on to captain Burnley to the League Championship in 1920-21 when the club set a record of thirty unbeaten games in a season that was not surpassed until the Arsenal 'Invincibles' in 2003-04. He ended his playing career at Wrexham and afterwards had a coaching spell in Germany. In 2010 Barnsley and Burnley football clubs jointly commissioned a stone for the previously unmarked final resting place of their joint legend.

| | League | | FA Cup | |
	App	Gls	App	Gls
1906-1907	26		5	
1907-1908	31	1	1	
1908-1909	32	6	1	
1909-1910	32	7	9	1
1910-1911	30	2	2	1
1911-1912	5	1		
Totals	156	17	18	2

5. BRATLEY, Philip Wright
1910-14   121 appearances and 8 Goals
Born. 26 December 1880, Rawmarsh
Ht 5'10" Wt 11-7
Centre-half/Right or Left-half
Rawmarsh to 1902; then Doncaster Rovers (3 appearances), Rotherham Town, Rotherham County; May 1910 BARNSLEY; May1914 Liverpool (13 appearances); 1919 Rotherham County (10 appearances);1921 Worksop Town.
Barnsley debut: aged 29 years 272 days, away to Blackpool, 24 September 1910 (lost 2-1)

Played 1912 Final
After playing for a number of local clubs Phil signed for Barnsley just five days after the 1910 final but he was not taken on the European tour. Reports of the time recall the 'youngster's' signing and the subsequent season saw him playing as a reserve and deputising for the half-back line. Whether the club officials regarded Phil as one for the future is unknown but despite his youthful looks the truth of the matter was he was approaching his 30th

Phil Bratley.
Wood Collection

birthday. The transfer of captain and club favourite Tommy Boyle to Burnley in 1911 saw Edward Hanlon tried in the centre-half position and when he picked up an injury Phil began an extended run in the first team. His inclusion coincided with a transformation in the club's form as Barnsley went on to lose just once in his first twenty-seven games. He remained an ever present in the cup side with a personal highlight of heading the winning goal in the semi-final replay against Swindon Town. He was also one of only two Yorkshiremen to play in the successful 1912 side. In the subsequent two seasons he missed just three games and in the two cup games against Liverpool in 1914 he was regarded as the best player on the pitch. There was little surprise when the Merseysiders announced his signing, along with fellow cup winner Wilf Bartrop, for the 1914-15 season but it remains unknown if they knew their capture was approaching thirty-four. In the final season before the suspension of the league due to the war, Phil made just thirteen appearances for the Anfield club, including playing in the infamous match against Manchester United. Leading players in both camps were found guilty of fixing the result of the match and seven of their number received life bans from the FA but Phil was not implicated in the matter. After the war he rejoined Rotherham County for their first season of league football and called time on his professional career at the age of forty.

	League		FA Cup	
	App	Gls	App	Gls
1910-1911	12			
1911-1912	19		12	1
1912-1913	36	5	3	
1913-1914	37	2	2	
Totals	104	7	17	1

6. COOPER (HOLLOWAY), John Denman
1908-15   192 appearances
Born: 25 February 1887, Sneinton
Ht 5'10^{1}/$_{2}$" Wt 12-5
Goalkeeper
Sutton Town; April 1908 BARNSLEY; 1919 Newport County (81 appearances)
Barnsley debut: aged 21 years 234 days, home against Glossop, 17 October 1908 (lost 3-1)

Played 1912 Final

Jack was a goalkeeping native of Nottingham who signed for the club in April 1908 from Sutton Town for £20. He was christened with the surname Holloway and it still has not been established why he chose the name Cooper throughout his career. Although he was only brought in as back up to Tommy Thorpe, his signing was reflective of the strength in depth at the club and prior to the start of the 1908-09 season the directors announced they had secured 'the most likely set of men who have ever worn the Oakwell colours'. His first season comprised almost totally of reserve football bar a few sporadic first team outings, but the transfer of Thorpe to Southern League Northampton opened the way to a regular place. He remained an ever-present up until Christmas 1909 when a serious injury picked up in the Derby County game threatened to end his career. He made two attempts at a comeback including a couple of appearances in the cup run of 1910 but it took just short of two years for Jack to achieve full fitness. His return in November 1911 coincided with a serious injury to John Clegg and he went on to

Jackie Cooper.
Wood Collection

hold the goalkeeping jersey until the suspension of the Leagues in 1915. As well as being a cup winner in 1912 he went on to make a total of 157 consecutive appearances which remained an Oakwell record until being surpassed by Harry Hough some forty years later. During the hostilities he served in the Royal Field Artillery in France for two years and had it not been for the war he would have pushed this record further. Indeed, in the three seasons after its end, he missed just six games but by this time he was playing for Newport County. During his time in Wales he famously threw the ball in his own net in one game and, after being pelted with missiles at Millwall, he entered the crowd to 'sort the situation out'. This resulted with him being flattened by a useful right hook and 'The Den' being closed for a fortnight by the football authorities. He also reputedly spent his spare time poaching, which he passed on to his fellow players, and was a keen racing man making him a well known face on Nottingham racecourse.

	League		FA Cup	
	App	Gls	App	Gls
1908-1909	8			
1909-1910	25		2	
1910-1911				
1911-1912	25		12	
1912-1913	38		3	
1913-1914	38		2	
1914-1915	38		1	
Totals	172		20	

7. DOWNS, John (Dickie) Thomas
1908-20   308 appearances and 11 Goals

Born: 13 August 1886, Middridge
Ht 5'7^1/$_2$" Wt 12-0
Right-back/Left-back
Crook Town, Shildon Athletic; May1908 BARNSLEY; March 1920 Everton (92 appearances); 1924 Brighton & Hove Albion (16 appearances)
Barnsley debut: aged 22 years 20 days, away to Blackpool, 2 September 1908 (drew 1-1)

Played 1910 and 1912 Finals

Quite a few sources credit 'Dickie' with the forename Richard but the truth of the matter is that his nickname came from the slang music hall term for a man's appendage. He was a tough-tackling, speedy full-back who is sometimes credited in inventing the sliding tackle. He joined the ranks at Oakwell in May 1908 and was an ever-present in his first season of professional football and went on became the first Barnsley footballer to receive national recognition when he was selected for the Football League just two weeks before the 1910 final. After the Cup success of 1912, he was selected, along with George Utley, to represent 'The North' against England in an International trial game. The game resulted in a 5-0 win for the

Northerners but only Utley was selected for the forthcoming Ireland game. Dickie had many chances to leave Barnsley for the First Division but preferred to stay at the club in the hope of winning promotion with the Reds. He lost four of his potentially best years due to World War One but the resumption of competition saw him reach a couple of milestones. First of all, he overtook Albert Oxsprings' appearance record for the club and eight games later he became the first Barnsley player to make 300 appearances. In 1920, following an early exit in the cup, he received and accepted an offer to join Everton and finally achieved his ambition of playing top flight football. His first season was very successful, a fact that did not go unnoticed by the international selectors and just seven months after leaving Oakwell he won his one and only cap for England, against Ireland, aged thirty-four. After four full seasons at Goodison Park he saw out his career on the south coast, playing for Brighton & Hove Albion. Charlie Buchan, the former Arsenal player and later football writer

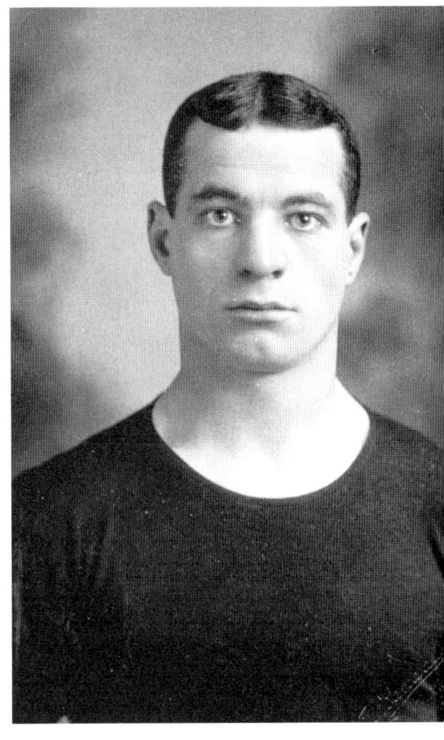

Dickie Downs.
Wood Collection

mentioned the legacy of Dickie Downs in his autobiography. He commented that the sliding tackle he introduced although completely legal had increased the amount of physical contact in the game and altered its character for ever.

| | League | | FA Cup | |
	App	Gls	App	Gls
1908-1909	38		1	
1909-1910	31		9	
1910-1911	37		2	
1911-1912	37		12	
1912-1913	37		3	
1913-1914	31	2	2	
1914-1915	37	6	1	
No Competition due to World War One				
1919-1920	28	2	2	1
Totals	276	10	32	1

8. FORMAN, Thomas (Tom/Tommy)
1907-11   136 Appearances 18 Goals

Born: 26 October 1879, Basford
Ht 5'7$^{1}/_{2}$" Wt 11-12
Outside-left
August 1900 Nottingham Forest (5 appearances); April 1902 Manchester City; Sutton Town; May1907 BARNSLEY; February 1911 Tottenham Hotspur (8appearances 1 goal); June 1912 Sutton Junction
Barnsley debut: aged 27years 315 days, home to Clapton Orient, 5 September 1907 (drew 2-2)

Tom Forman.
Bower Collection

Played 1910 Final

Tommy signed for Barnsley in May 1907 from Sutton Town and immediately fitted into the gap at outside-left made by the vacating Joe Brooks. Earlier in his career he had tasted league football at Nottingham Forest where his brothers Frank and Fred had played with much distinction. Between them they played some 450 league games for the club and even represented England together, but Tom could only muster a handful of games before leaving. After a trial at Manchester City, he settled at Midland League Sutton Town and the further move to Oakwell saw him link up with former team mates Bill Collins and the prolific George Reeves. Throughout his time with the Reds he was never far from the first team and established a reputation as one as the quickest wingmen in the Second Division. He was never a prolific goal scorer but his telling crosses led to many a goal and were a major feature of the clubs play at the time. In the cup run of 1910 he did manage two goals on the way to the Final, with the strike in the Semi-Final against Everton being the most important. The following season saw the Reds struggle to find anything like their cup-tie form but Tommy was still a consistent performer, a fact that had not gone unnoticed. In February 1911, having played in all that seasons games, he was transferred to First Division Tottenham Hotspur. The move was to help the Londoners in their fight against relegation which proved successful, but in his two years at the club he featured in just eight games, mainly as back-up for the great Bert Middlemas. He ended his career back in Nottinghamshire playing for Sutton Junction.

	League		FA Cup	
	App	Gls	App	Gls
1907-1908	33	2	1	
1908-1909	34	4		
1909-1910	33	6	9	2
1910-1911	24	4	2	
Totals	124	16	12	2

9. GADSBY, Ernest
1909-1910   51 appearances and 16 goals

Born: circa 1884, New Whittington
Ht 5'6" Wt 11-6
Inside-right/Inside-left/Centre-forward
New Whittington Exchange; 1904 Chesterfield Town (15 appearances 2 goals); Denaby United, Mexborough Town; August 1909 BARNSLEY; December 1910 Bristol City (10 appearances 1 goal); Castleford Town; Worksop Town; c.1914 Glossop (32 appearances 5 goals); New Whittington Exchange; Clay Cross Town; Clay Cross Zingari; Bentley Colliery
Barnsley debut: home to Hull City, 2 September 1909 (lost 2-1)

Played 1910 Final

Ernest came from a large footballing family of eleven brothers who were well known in the North Derbyshire area. He had already tasted league football at Chesterfield, along with his brother Walter, prior to moving onto Midland League football. He joined the club in August 1909 from near neighbours Mexborough Town and was selected at inside-right for the opening game of the season against Hull. This berth had proved difficult to fill in the previous campaign with no fewer than seven players being tried in the position, so it was a great relief to the staff at Oakwell that Ernest proved an instant success. During a thirteen-game spell in the early part of the season, he hit nine goals, including a hat-trick against Wolves, in a 7-1 romp. During the cup run of 1910 he grabbed three goals including the important opener in the semi-final replay against Everton; and in the Final his accurate passing was deemed one of the features of the game. In the disastrous 1910/11 season he was the first member of the cup-final side to be moved on. The slump in form was difficult to pinpoint but after an initial period of being dropped from the side he was

Ernest Gadsby.
Bower Collection

swapped for Bristol City goalkeeper John Clegg in December 1910. The move to the First Division club was short-lived and after a spell back in local football he returned to the Football League with Glossop for the 1914-15 season. Finally, the Gadsby brothers once famously issued a challenge by means of the national press to play football against any other eleven brothers. Not surprisingly there were no takers.

| | League | | FA Cup | |
	App	Gls	App	Gls
1909-1910	33	12	9	3
1910-1911	9	1		
Totals	42	13	9	3

10. GLENDENNING, Robert
1907-1913   170 appearances and 1 goal

Born: 6 June 1888, Harraton
Ht 5'7" Wt 11-7
Right-half
Washington United; April 1907 BARNSLEY; March 1913 Bolton Wanderers (73 appearances); 1919 Accrington Stanley
Barnsley debut: aged 18 years 323 days, away to West Bromwich Albion, 25 April 1907 (lost 3-1)

Played 1910 and 1912 Finals

Bob Glendenning first came to Oakwell as an amateur trialist in the final weeks of the 1906-7 season. Although he would become one of the most distinguished defenders to have played for the club, his trial appearance was in the forward line. He was selected for the final League game of the season at West Bromwich Albion and his performance that day was compared to the English international and former Barnsley favourite George Wall. Needless to say, the committee moved quickly to secure his services for the forthcoming season. His first year as a professional comprised almost entirely of reserve team football as he played understudy to Tommy Boyle and Fred Tomlinson but the following campaign saw Bob become a feature in the first team. Initially providing cover for the injured Boyle, he deputised with such conviction that Tommy was switched to centre-half on his return to fitness and the popular defender Billy Silto was allowed to leave the club.

He was an ever-present in the cup-runs of 1910 and 1912 and his incisive pass in the Bramall Lane Final allowed Harry Tufnell to race clear and score the winner. In March 1913, despite the Reds being handily placed in the table, they accepted a big money offer from First Division Bolton Wanderers for his services. The fee of £1,200 was fractionally smaller than that received for Boyle in 1911 and it was significant in that this marked the first sale of a member of the successful cup-winning side. At Bolton, he was immediately made club captain and what would have been a glorious career at Burnden Park was cut short by the First World War. He played just 73 games and after the War had a spell at Accrington Stanley before retiring from the game. A move to Holland saw a successful period of coaching where from 1925 onwards he acted as coach to both Koninklijke HFC and the Dutch national team. After the 1928 Olympics he decided to focus his attentions solely on the national side and held the position until 1940, when he escaped the Nazi invasion of Holland by a matter of a few hundred yards. He managed the Oranje at the World Cups of 1934 and 1938 with little success but his record as manager still shows the greatest number of victories. In recognition of the part he played in the country's football history, the Dutch Football Association pays for the upkeep of his grave in Bolton.

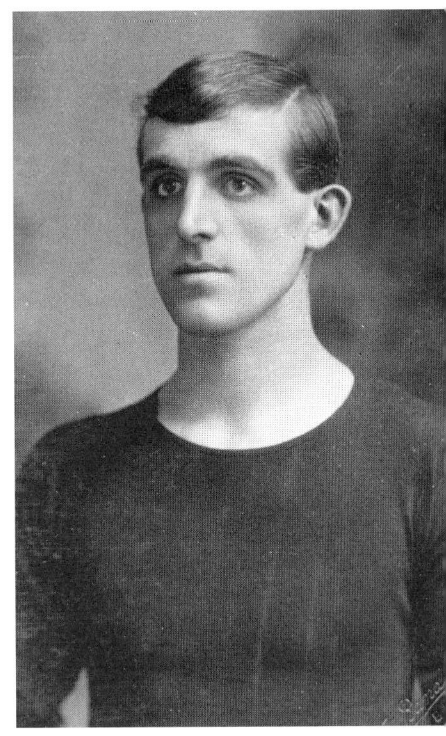

Bob Glendenning.
Wood Collection

| | League | | FA Cup | |
	App	Gls	App	Gls
1906-1907	1			
1907-1908	1			
1908-1909	19		1	
1909-1910	33		9	
1910-1911	30		2	
1911-1912	32	1	12	
1912-1913	27		3	
Totals	**143**	**1**	**27**	

11. LEAVEY, Herbert James
1911-12   34 Appearances 3 Goals

Born: 5 May 1886, Guildford
Ht 5'9¹/₂" Wt 11-2
Outside-left
Woodland Villa; Plymouth Argyle; 1908 Derby County; Plymouth Argyle; 1910 Liverpool (5 appearances), Aug1911 BARNSLEY, cs1913 Bradford Park Avenue(19a 1g), Llanelli, Mar1921 Portsmouth(13a 0g), Boscombe,

Barnsley debut aged 25yrs 120 days away Huddersfield Town 2-Sep-1911 lost 2-1

Bert Leavey.
Wood Collection

Played in the 1912 campaign

Bert joined Barnsley in August 1911 from Liverpool having played just a handful games for the Anfield club. He was brought in to fill the void left by Tom Forman's move to Tottenham and from the opening day was a constant feature on the left side of the attack. In the Fourth Round second replay against Bradford City he suffered an unfortunate double fracture of his leg which ended his Barnsley career. Such was the chaos of the occasion, with the gates being rushed several times and constant crowd encroachment onto the pitch, that the provision of Ambulancemen had being completely overlooked. Leavey had to be carried from the field in the arms of a few men. Three days later Jimmy Moore who had only played previously on the right was selected for the replay and kept his place right through to the final and beyond. The club obviously held Bert in high esteem and after the victorious cup win they paid for an additional winner's medal to be presented to the winger.

Also they arranged that the cup-winning bonus of £25 that was awarded to the players should be split equally between himself and Jimmy Moore. At the beginning of the next season he was made available for transfer for a sum of £150 but there were no takers and he spent a frustrating year trying to displace the impressive Moore. In the summer of 1913 he eventually moved on to Bradford Park Avenue, playing nineteen games in his only season and helping the club to win promotion to the First Division for the first time in their history. He later had spells as player-manager of

Llanelli and Boscombe FC, and after the war he coached extensively in Holland at the insistence of Bob Glendenning; and from 1933 to 1952 was manager of the Helder Racing Club.

| | League | | FA Cup | |
	App	Gls	App	Gls
1911-1912	27	2	7	1
Totals	27	2	7	1

12. LILLYCROP, George Beanland
1907-1913   224 appearances 104 goals
Born: 17 December 1886, Alverstoke
Ht 5'6^1/$_2$" Wt 11-4
Centre-forward
South Shields Adelaide; North Shields Athletic; May1907 BARNSLEY; Aug1913 Bolton Wanderers (52 appearances 31 goals);1919 South Shields (44 appearances 16 goals)
Barnsley debut: aged 20 years 313 days, away to Oldham Athletic, 26 October 1907 (lost 1-0)

Played 1910 and 1912 Finals
George signed professional forms for the club prior to the 1907-08 season and was initially brought in to provide competition for the centre-forward position with Natty Hellewell and Ernie McShea. He joined from Northern League North Shields Athletic and had to wait until October to make his debut when an injury to Hellewell gave him his chance. A further injury to McShea gave him an extended run in the team but a return of no goals in his first ten games gave no indication that George would go on to break all goal scoring records at the club. His nineteen goals in 1908-09 equalled Harry Swann's tally for a season and included hat-tricks against Blackpool and Chesterfield. The twenty-five goals he scored the following campaign remained a record until 1933-4 when Abe Blight surpassed it scoring

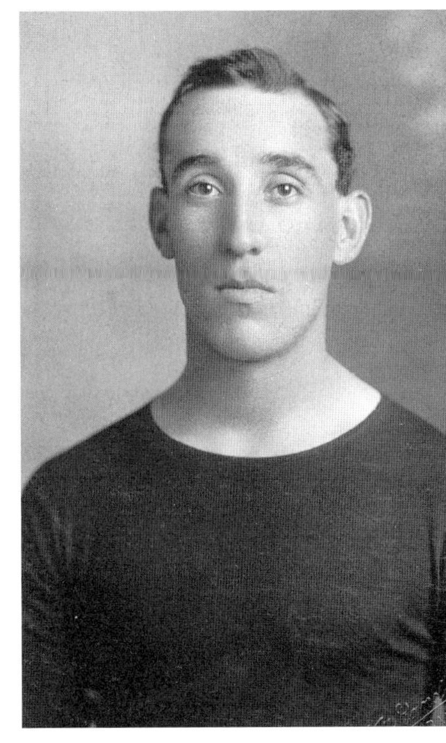

George Lillycrop.
Wood Collection

thirty-one times as the club won its first Division Three North title. He was an ever present in the Cup runs of 1910 and 1912, and after twenty-four goals in 1912-13 he followed the influential Bob Glendenning in moving from Oakwell to Bolton Wanderers. The fee of £1,300 was a record for Barnsley, beating Tommy Boyle's move to Burnley in 1912; but the loss of their most natural goal scorer was almost too much to take for the fans as they were seeing the great side of 1912 being sold off before their eyes. His 104 goals for the club is second only to Ernest Hine and he remains one of only three players to have scored twenty-plus goals in two different seasons. At Burnden Park he continued his prolific strike rate, grabbing thirty-one goals in fifty-two games before the First World War brought a close to his top flight career. After the war, and in the twilight of his career, he returned to South Shields to score sixteen goals in forty-four games before retiring and taking up a coaching role. Finally, after over fifteen years as coach to South Shields, Gateshead and Bradford City, he was appointed manager at Crewe Alexandria in 1938.

| | League | | FA Cup | |
	App	Gls	App	Gls
1907-1908	27	9	1	
1908-1909	32	18	1	1
1909-1910	32	23	9	2
1910-1911	34	11	2	1
1911-1912	33	9	12	6
1912-1913	38	22	3	2
Totals	196	92	28	12

13. MEARNS, Frederick Charles
1909-10 34 appearances
Born: 31 March 1879, Sunderland
Ht 5'9½" Wt 12-7
Goalkeeper
Selbourne; Whitburn; January 1901 Sunderland (2 appearances); May 1902 Kettering Town; March 1903 Tottenham Hotspur; May 1904 Bradford City (21 appearances); 1905 Grays United; December 1905 Southern United; March 1906 Barrow; May 1906 Bury (10 appearances); 1908 Hartlepool United; July 1909 BARNSLEY; January 1911 Leicester Fosse (68 appearances); Newcastle City; Sunderland West End

Fred Mearns.
Bower Collection

Barnsley debut: aged 30 years 276 days, away to Stockport County, 1 January 1910 (lost 5-0)

Played 1910 Final

Fred was a much-travelled goalkeeper whose first job in professional football was at his hometown club of Sunderland, as understudy to Scottish international Ned Doig. A move to Southern League Kettering saw him reputedly save nineteen penalty kicks in barely one season and six further moves in six years saw him arrive at Oakwell in time for the 1909-10 season. Initially just signed as a back up, a serious injury to Jackie Cooper in December 1909 gave Fred a free run at the first team and the chance of a cup-winner's medal. Probably his best game for the club came in the semi-final replay with Everton when, with the scores tied at 0-0, he saved a penalty to keep the Reds in the game. The following season saw Fred and the club fail dramatically to produce anything like the form that had taken them to the Final. Cooper's injury showed no sign of improving so moves were made to sign another keeper, with John Clegg of Bristol City being engaged. Immediately, Fred was dropped and after six weeks in the reserves he was swapped for Leicester Fosse's equally nomadic George Travers. After two and a half years service at Filbert Street he moved back to the North East, with Newcastle City and later he acted as trainer to Durham City. He was described as 'A cool, calculating and level-headed player, wonderfully active, and clears low shots with ease' but a *Leicester Mail* testimonial also put it that Fred 'carries a left-hand punch that Jack Johnson might envy'. He was a carpenter by trade and when he joined Hartlepools as their first professional player he was set the task of bringing the ground up to scratch in the summer months.

| | League | | FA Cup | |
	App	Gls	App	Gls
1909-1910	13		7	
1910-1911	14			
Totals	27		7	

14. MOORE, James
1911-1914   111 appearances 24 goals

Born: 1 September 1891, Felling-on-Tyne
Ht 5'8½" Wt 11-0
Inside-left/Outside-left/Centre-forward
Boldon Colliery Welfare; August 1911 BARNSLEY; 1919 Southampton(42 appearances 12 goals); 1921 Leeds United (27 appearances 4 goals); 1922 Brighton & Hove Albion (6 appearances 2 goals); 1923 Halifax Town (40 appearances 7 goals); 1924 Queen's Park Rangers (26 appearances 5 goals); 1925 Crewe Alexandra (13 appearances 6 goals)
Barnsley debut: aged 20 years 36 days, away to Bradford Park Avenue, 7 October 1911 (lost 1-0)

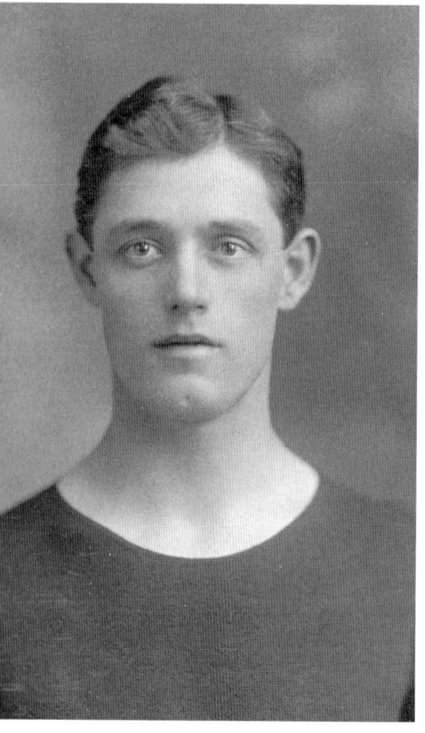

Jimmy Moore.
Wood Collection

Played 1912 Final

Jimmy joined Barnsley prior to the start of the 1911-12 season and was the youngest and least experienced of the side that won the cup. The first six months of his debut professional season was as back-up for Wilf Bartrop on the right wing, and after making his senior bow at Bradford Park Avenue in October he had just six games under his belt by mid-March. The turning point came after the FA Cup 4th round second replay against Bradford City when a serious injury to Bert Leavey effectively ended his career. Three days later, Barnsley tried the bold experiment of playing the right-footed Moore on the left-wing in the third replay at Bramall Lane and it was an unmitigated success. He was described in the press as 'showing speed, skill, accuracy and strength in shooting' and it was noted in the way he was fearless in facing his burly opponent Campbell. From that moment he was an ever-present in the side and was one of only four players to have played in all the twelve games in twenty-six days of April 1912. He was never a prolific scorer but he did grab Barnsley's goal in the 'Champions of the World' game with Celtic, thanks to a 'gem of a shot' and in 1913-14, when he totalled thirteen goals for the season, he hit a hat-trick against Grimsby Town. Like most of his generation he the lost the prime of his career to the First World War but still managed to be a regular in the side at Oakwell, despite being employed in a factory making aeroplanes on the Isle of Wight. Between 1915 and 1919 he played forty-three games, scoring twenty-two goals and he also guested for Southern League Southampton. Prior to the

1919-20 season he returned to Oakwell, only to be told he was no longer required and within hours had secured a deal with the Saints. The following season he was a member of their first ever Football League side against Gillingham. Several moves followed his spell on the south coast, including a period coaching in Holland at the insistence of Bob Glendenning, but he had married a Barnsley girl so it was only natural he would eventually move back to the area. His connection with the Oakwell club was re-established after the Second World War when he became a director. His nephew Ralph Potter and subsequently his son Ian continued to be members of the board up until October 2002.

| | League | | FA Cup | |
	App	Gls	App	Gls
1911-1912	16	1	5	
1912-1913	33	5	2	1
1913-1914	34	13	1	
1914-1915	20	4		
Totals	103	23	8	1

15. NESS, Harold Marshall
1908-1911   78 appearances
Born: circa 1885, Scarborough
Ht 5′9″ Wt 12-9
Left-back
Sheffield; Parkgate; Rawmarsh Athletic; May 1908 BARNSLEY; July 1912 Sunderland (94 appearances); 1920 Aberdeen
Barnsley debut: away to Burnley, 5 December 1908 (lost 3-2)

Played 1910 Final
Harry joined the club in the summer of 1908 having played local amateur football but the excellent full-back pairing of Jack Little and Dickie Downs limited his first team appearances to just three games. The following campaign saw him replace Little at left-back for the opening game of the season and he quickly looked the finished article and being totally suited to the demands of the position. He was described in the local press as 'having superb judgement' and such was the 'marked coolness' in his performances

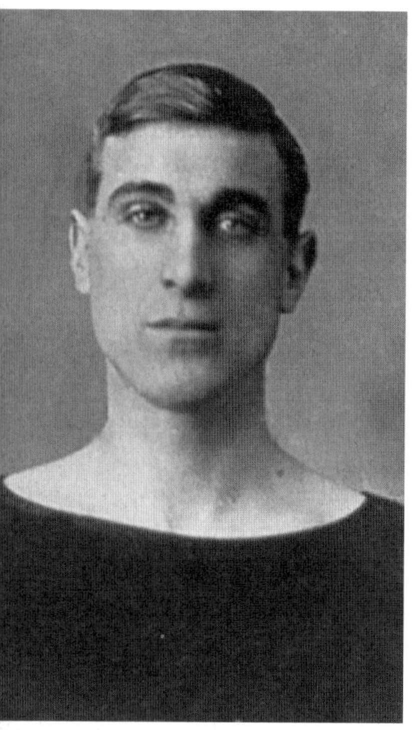

Harry Ness.
Bower Collection

that he remained an immediate first team selection for his remaining time at the club. After the disappointment of the Cup Final defeat he played throughout the disastrous re-election season of 1910-11 to a level that attracted the attention of First Division Sunderland. A summer move to Roker should have opened wonderful new chapter in his career but he struggled to displace former Barnsley defender Albert Milton from the full-back berth. The 1912-13 season proved to be one of their most successful in the Black Cats' history but it took a serious injury to Milton to give Harry a run in the side. He was recalled to the team for a successful FA Cup semi-final victory and one month later he received a second cup-loser's medal after a 1-0 defeat by Aston Villa. Any disappointment he may have felt was short lived as four days later a draw in the League at Aston Villa would be enough to win Sunderland the title and Harry a Championship medal. After the war he returned to Roker Park but was unable to command a first team place and after a few months moved on to Aberdeen where he ended his playing career.

| | League | | FA Cup | |
	App	Gls	App	Gls
1908-1909	3			
1909-1910	35		9	
1910-1911	29		2	
Totals	67		11	

16. TAYLOR, Archibald
1911-1912   71 appearances
Born: 28 November 1879, Dundee
Ht 5'9$^{1}/_{2}$" Wt 13-0
Left-back/Right-back
1904 Bolton Wanderers (3 appearances); Bristol Rovers; Brentford; West Ham United; Dundee;

Falkirk; 1910 Huddersfield Town (29 appearances); August 1911 BARNSLEY; 1914 York City

Barnsley debut: aged 31years 279 days, away to Huddersfield Town, 2 September 1911 (lost 2-1)

Played 1912 Final

Archie arrived at Oakwell in August 1911 from Huddersfield Town as a direct replacement for Harry Ness who had joined First Division Sunderland. He was a strong, no-nonsense Scot, who brought to the club a wealth of experience, and when Tommy Boyle was sold to Burnley in October 1911 he was the natural selection to be club captain. He fitted in perfectly with Downs, Utley, Bratley and Glendenning to form a solid brick wall of a defence, and from his left back berth he marshalled the team to the Final success at Bramall Lane. In the Final he was noted for keeping the West Bromwich winger Jephcott in check and at its conclusion he received the Cup on behalf of the club from Mr JC Clegg, the FA President. On returning to Barnsley, he had the embarrassment of having the trophy knocked from his grasp and under the feet of an accompanying horse. The 'Old Tin Pot' suffered a small amount of damage for which the FA dutifully billed the club for its repair. The following season as the club hoped to make a serious promotion push, Archie broke his leg against Leicester Fosse and ended up spending four weeks in Barnsley's Beckett Hospital. His place in the side was filled by John Bethune and, although the injury was not as bad as first thought, he spent fifteen months on the sidelines before moving on. He accepted the role of secretary-manager at York City in 1914 but found himself out of the game during the war years and on resumption of football he served Birmingham City for many years as trainer.

In April 2010, a group of Barnsley historians traced the final resting place of Archie to the Scone cemetery, near Perth in Scotland. The gravestone failed to acknowledge his burial and when this fact was brought to the attention of Barnsley Football Club they immediately agreed to commission an inscription.

Archie Taylor.
Wood Collection

	League		FA Cup	
	App	Gls	App	Gls
1911-1912	33		12	
1912-1913	23		3	
Totals	56		15	

17. TRAVERS, George Edward
1911-1914   99 appearances 25 goals

Born: Jul/Aug 1887, London
Ht 5'7$^{1}/_{2}$" Wt 11-12
Inside-right/Centre-forward
Bilston United; Rowley United; July 1906 Wolverhampton Wanderers; August 1907 Birmingham (2 appearances); December 1908 Aston Villa (4 appearances 4 goals); May 1909 Queen's Park Rangers; August 1910 Leicester Fosse (12 appearances 5 goals); January 1911 BARNSLEY; February 1914 Manchester United (21 appearances 4 goals); 1919 Swindon Town; June 1920 Millwall Athletic (2 appearances); October 1920 Norwich City (29 appearances 14 goals); June 1921 Gillingham (10 appearances 1 goal); Nuneaton Town; November 1922 Cradley Heath St. Luke's; Bilston United;

George Travers.
Wood Collection

Barnsley debut: away to Clapton Orient, 21 January 1911 (lost 3-0)

Played 1912 Final

George was the son of the music hall comedian Hyram Travers and like his father had a nomadic existence throughout his career. He arrived at Oakwell in January 1911 from Leicester Fosse in a straight swap for goalkeeper Fred Mearns but managed just seven games in his first year as the club struggled to find an inside-right in form. In December 1911 he was recalled to the side at the expense of Fred Martin and went on to miss just one of the remaining league and cup games. Included in this spell was a hectic period of twelve games in twenty-six days in April as the club tried to win the cup and deal with a fixture backlog. Probably his most important goal for the club came in the FA Cup 4th round third replay with Bradford City when his smart shot set the way for a 3-2 victory. It was the first goal City had conceded in twelve FA Cup games which remains a shut-out record to this day. In the 1912-13 season he scored a career best of ten goals for the season as Barnsley finished in fourth position and the following campaign he had equalled this amount by January before being transferred out. His three-year spell at the Oakwell turned out to be the longest stay at any of his clubs and the move to Manchester United saw him link up with former favourites George Wall and George Stacey. Throughout his career and later life George was always a colourful character and served several prison sentences and immigrated to New Zealand twice. In July 1912 he lost his cup winner's medal in Barnsley and in circumstances that were never fully explained it was returned to him anonymously by post.

	League		FA Cup	
	App	Gls	App	Gls
1910-1911	5			
1911-1912	22	4	12	1
1912-1913	35	10	3	
1913-1914	20	9	2	1
Totals	82	23	17	2

18. TUFNELL, Harry
1909-1920   230 appearances 70 goals
Born: 2 March 1886, Burton-on-Trent
Ht 5'7½" Wt 11-0
Inside-left/Inside-right
Worcester City; 1907 Bury (13 appearances 3 goals); July 1909 BARNSLEY; Wakefield City; Doncaster Rovers
Barnsley debut: aged 23 years 186 days, away to Glossop, 4 September 1909 (lost 3-0)

Played 1910 and 1912 Finals
Harry signed for the club in the summer of 1909 from First Division Bury where in the previous twelve months he had scored just one goal in three games. He didn't make the side for the opening game of the season but was selected two days later at Glossop and went on to become a permanent fixture in the inside-left position. He returned a modest seven goals for his thirty-one league games in his first season but it was in the FA cup that he saved his best, grabbing six goals in nine games. Not only did he score the winner in a third round clash with West Bromwich, he hit the clinching goal in the Semi-Final

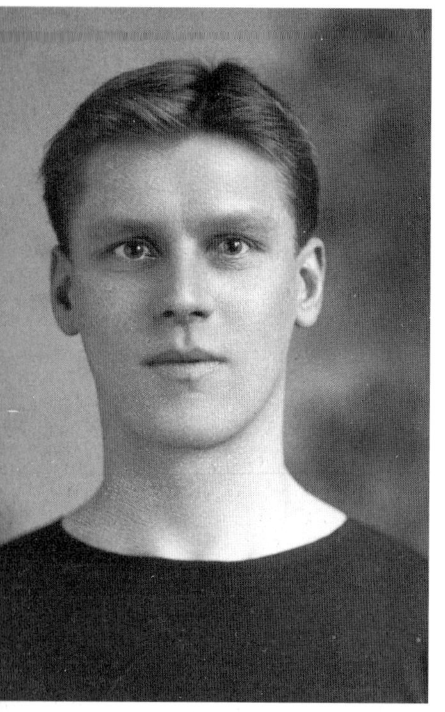

Harry Tufnell.
Wood Collection

with Everton and got what looked like the winning goal in the Final with Newcastle until a late equaliser forced a replay. So late was this goal that the wife of Arthur Fairclough had given up her red ribbons to be tied to the trophy. The following season saw Harry record a career high of fourteen goals as the club embarrassingly had to apply for re-election but it is for the 1911-12 campaign that he is to be best remembered. He scored thirteen goals in the cup-winning season, all of them individual strikes, but none so important as the winning goal in the Final. Entering into the last minute of extra-time, he received the ball from Glendenning, beat the England defender Pennington with a single touch and then chipped the advancing keeper. He was congratulated by his team mates including Glendenning who excitedly knocked him to the floor and clean bit through his ear. As the blood started to poor down from the wound the right-half commented: 'Tha' can put a ring in thee'er, Tuffy'. It's not recorded if Harry took up the advice but he had become a part of Barnsley folklore from that goal onwards. In the subsequent seasons he played and scored regularly until the First World War halted his career but he was still around in 1919 to play a few games although at centre-half. After leaving Oakwell in the summer of 1920 he served as player-manager to both Wakefield City and Doncaster Rovers before spending many seasons as trainer to Oldham Athletic.

| | League | | FA Cup | |
	App	Gls	App	Gls
1909-1910	31	7	9	6
1910-1911	33	14	2	
1911-1912	34	11	12	2
1912-1913	35	9	3	2
1913-1914	26	8	2	
1914-1915	37	9	1	
Competition cancelled due to WW1				
1919-1920	5	2		
Totals	201	60	29	10

19. UTLEY, George
1908-1914   193 appearances 9 goals

Born: 16 May 1887 Elsecar
Ht 5'8$\frac{1}{2}$" Wt 13-0
Left-half
Elsecar; Wentworth FC; 1906 Sheffield Wednesday; Elsecar; January 1908 BARNSLEY; November 1913 Sheffield United (107 appearances 4 goals); 1922 Manchester City (1 appearance)
Barnsley debut: aged 20 years 340 days, away to West Bromwich Albion, 20 April 1908 (drew 1-1)

Played 1910 and 1912 Finals

George followed his older brother Erwin to Oakwell after playing in local football and signed a professional contract at the club on New Year's Day 1908. He made his debut towards the end of the season replacing the Billy Silto at West Bromwich and the following year was spent as understudy to the half-back line where he managed fourteen games. On the opening day of the 1909-10 season he replaced the veteran Albert Oxspring at left-half to form a back line that could be both ruthless and creative. All three members had come through the ranks and together with Bob Glendenning and captain Tommy Boyle, its elder statesman at the ripe old age of twenty-four years, they formed a solid defensive unit. George's strength came in that not only was he a great defender and organiser like his two team mates but he was also a useful dribbler with a tremendous shot. These qualities were recognised in the season after the cup success when he was selected to play for England in a trial game against

George Utley.
Wood Collection

the South. He ended up on the losing side but in January 1913 he was chosen for another trial game, this time against England for 'The North'. He was joined in the side by Dickie Downs, Tommy Boyle and Jackie Mordue and the Northerners routed the opposition 5-0, with George grabbing the opening goal. Needless to say it was no surprise when the England team to meet Ireland was announced that George and Tommy were selected for their debuts. They were joined in the side by former Reds Mordue and Wall but Downs was unfortunately overlooked. On returning to Oakwell after the international, George was a proud and happy man and scored a remarkable free kick goal from the halfway line against Leicester Fosse but the game would be the last for the cup-winning side. Archie Taylor broke a leg at its conclusion and six days later Glendenning was sold to Bolton Wanderers. In the summer the Lancashire club added Lillycrop to their ranks and ten games into the new season they came for George. An offer of £1,500 was turned down by Barnsley but this alerted Sheffield United to his availability and, after a period of negotiation, a £2,000 bid from the Blades was accepted. The fee was a record for the game at that time but no amount of money would placate the angry Barnsley fans. The move came too soon on the back of the others and was taken as the final straw for many. He signed a long-term deal at Bramall Lane and captained the side to cup success in 1915, but missed the following four seasons due to the War. On the league's resumption in 1919 he continued his connection with the club but in 1922, when he was no longer an instant first team choice, he left the club for Manchester City.

| | League | | FA Cup | |
	App	Gls	App	Gls
1907-1908	1			
1908-1909	14	1		
1909-1910	35		9	1
1910-1911	36	1	2	
1911-1912	34	4	12	
1912-1913	36	1	3	
1913-1914	11	1		
Totals	167	8	26	1

Following on from the Utley transfer, there were many letters written to the press passing opinion on the move and the policy of the board in general. Below is how one fan summed up the situation giving an indication of how he and others felt.

'We have paid good money to see Barnsley Football Club this season and I now find it has been like paying for strawberries and cream and being served gooseberries and skimmed milk and we are expected to eat it and say nowt. I will never go to Oakwell again.'

The Final Whistle

It is almost unarguable that the greatest team that Barnsley Football Club have ever had represented the club in the 1909-10 and 1911-12 seasons. To have reached the final of the most prestigious tournament in the world on one occasion was memorable enough but to do so twice and win it in 1912 was a marvellous achievement. Whether any Barnsley side can in the future repeat the feat we cannot be sure, but it will take an almighty effort to equal the achievements of players such as Downs, Glendenning, Bartrop, Tufnell and Lillycrop.

The Cup Final teams, like its players, may have been consigned to history but like all true legends their names will never fade and they will always be remembered.

As such to all of them we raise a cheer.